THE END TIMES SURVIVAL GUIDE

THE
END
TIMES
SURVIVAL
GUIDE

TEN BIBLICAL STRATEGIES
FOR FAITH AND HOPE
IN THESE UNCERTAIN DAYS

MARK HITCHCOCK

TYNDALE
MOMENTUM®

The nonfiction imprint of
Tyndale House Publishers, Inc.

Visit Tyndale online at www.tyndale.com.

Visit Tyndale Momentum online at www.tyndalemomentum.com.

TYNDALE, Tyndale Momentum, and Tyndale's quill logo are registered trademarks of Tyndale House Publishers, Inc. The Tyndale Momentum logo is a trademark of Tyndale House Publishers, Inc. Tyndale Momentum is the nonfiction imprint of Tyndale House Publishers, Inc., Carol Stream, Illinois.

Published in association with the literary agency of William K. Jensen Literary Agency, 119 Bampton Court, Eugene, Oregon 97404.

For information about special discounts for bulk purchases, please contact Tyndale House Publishers at csresponse@tyndale.com, or call 1-800-323-9400.

Library of Congress Cataloging-in-Publication Data

Names: Hitchcock, Mark, date- author.
Title: The end times survival guide : ten biblical strategies for faith and hope in these uncertain days / Mark Hitchcock.
Description: Carol Stream, Illinois : Tyndale House Publishers, Inc., [2018] | Includes bibliographical references.
Identifiers: LCCN 2018017913 | ISBN 9781496414090 (sc)
Subjects: LCSH: Hope--Religious aspects--Christianity. | Christian life. | End of the world.
Classification: LCC BV4638 .H58 2018 | DDC 234/.2--dc23 LC record available at https://lccn.loc.gov/2018017913

Printed in the United States of America

24   23   22   21   20   19   18
7   6   5   4   3   2   1

CONTENTS

ULTIMATE SURVIVOR

The future, like everything else, is not what it used to be.

PAUL VALÉRY

SURVIVAL IS BIG BUSINESS. Everywhere you look these days, someone is talking about survival. Entertainment outlets and the media have seized the survival craze.

The initial offering in the new survival genre, and reality TV, was the series *Survivor*, which premiered in the United States in 2000. The series features a group of strangers marooned at an isolated location where they have to scrounge for food, water, shelter, and fire. The show completed its thirty-fifth season in 2017. *Survivor* is the quintessential survivor in the media industry. Since *Survivor*, a steady stream of movies and series has focused on surviving in almost every possible predicament, including in a postapocalyptic world.

A spate of survival reality TV shows has also erupted. Consider these:

> *Out of the Wild: The Alaska Experiment*
> *Extreme Survival*

> *Man vs. Wild*
> *Survive This*
> *Fat Guys in the Woods*
> *Survivorman*
> *Surviving Disaster*
> *Dual Survival*
> *The Wheel*

Doomsday Preppers is another offering that demonstrates how to survive various doomsday scenarios. The survival business is booming online with all kinds of products designed to enhance a person's ability to endure any conceivable disruption, from living off the grid to all-out apocalypse. You can learn survival tips and buy survival gear for any eventuality. Online you can find all kinds of survival gurus touting their tips for surviving everything from school shootings to nuclear holocaust.

What's behind the survival obsession? Why are these programs, products, and pointers so successful? Because the future has never been more uncertain. Never more unknown. Never more unpredictable. We live in a world that seems to be on the verge of coming apart.

In 2017, a Las Vegas shooting spree at an outdoor concert left dozens massacred, a terrorist plowed through innocent pedestrians in New York City, and a gunman opened fire on a church service in a small Texas town, all in a little over a month. Evil is intensifying.

Political rancor and polarization in American politics has

shifted to another gear. Both sides are so entrenched that for someone to give any ground or to compromise in the least is viewed as total capitulation, making that person an outcast from all groups. Even commonsense solutions seem unachievable. The anger and outright malice on cable news and social media is over the top. Increasingly, protests fill the streets. Violence and racial tension are boiling over. Anarchy threatens. The family is in dire trouble. Deadly diseases and viruses like Ebola and Zika erupt with frightening regularity and can spread globally very quickly. Cataclysmic weather events seem to be escalating in frequency and intensity.

Beyond these things, the once faraway threat of a terrorist attack has jumped into everyone's life—the World Trade Center, the Pentagon, a subway in London, a train in Spain, a convention in California, a tourist hot spot in France, a nightclub in Orlando, a Christmas market in Berlin. No one seems safe anywhere. Millions of displaced, devastated people are fleeing their homelands, potentially giving terrorists cover to blend into and infiltrate Western nations.

Rogue regimes such as North Korea already have the bomb, and other nations like Iran are on the threshold. Barbaric terrorists threaten our safety and very way of life. Even as the caliphate is crumbling and ISIS is on the run, fleeing ISIS fighters are exporting their savagery to more locations. ISIS-inspired killers are hiding among us. There seems to be a collective, growing sense that things can't go on this way much longer.

And then there's the world economy, which, while doing

well on many fronts, seems increasingly fragile, susceptible at any time to a geopolitical crisis. The United States is twenty trillion dollars in debt, and that number is climbing. The debt bomb must explode at some point, triggering financial Armageddon.

In addition to all these things, there's an increasing indifference and malaise—and sometimes outright militancy—toward the central truths of the Christian faith and practice. Anti-Christian momentum is palpable. Hate and hostility toward Bible-believing Christians is on the rise. Christians are taking fire. Believers who dare even to question the legitimacy of same-sex marriage and gender fluidity are labeled "haters" and "homophobes." Believers in Jesus Christ now find themselves playing in enemy territory in American culture, and the crowd is getting more and more hostile.

Pornography is metastasizing like a deadly cancer and infecting an entire generation of young men and women. The young are swallowing a deadly cocktail of toxic ideas in the name of love and tolerance. We have front-row seats to a moral freefall. We're waiting for the other shoe to drop. Time seems to be running out.

What can we do?

ARE WE LIVING IN THE LAST DAYS?

Many of us have probably asked ourselves at some point whether we're living in the last days. Maybe we've asked it more often in recent times. When we ask about living in the last days, what we're really asking is "Are we living in the final days before the apocalypse? Is this the end of the age predicted in the Bible?"

In the New Testament, the term "last days" (or "last times") refers most often to the last days of the church on earth or this current age (see 1 Timothy 4:1; 2 Timothy 3:1; James 5:3; 1 Peter 1:20; 2 Peter 3:3).

All the way back in the first century, the apostle Peter said, "The end of the world is coming soon" (1 Peter 4:7). Even in New Testament times the apostles "sensed that they had moved dramatically closer to the consummation of God's plan for this world."[1] The Old Testament age had ended; they were now living in a brand-new era. For the apostles, the end of the age was already a present reality. The Scriptures indicate that the first coming of Jesus Christ inaugurated the "last days" for the church. According to the New Testament, we are living right now in these last days: "Now in these final [last] days, he has spoken to us through his Son. God promised everything to the Son as an inheritance, and through the Son he created the universe" (Hebrews 1:2).

The apostle John even calls this present age "the last hour": "Dear children, the last hour is here. You have heard that the Antichrist is coming, and already many such antichrists have appeared. From this we know that the last hour has come" (1 John 2:18). According to the New Testament, the last days commenced with Christ's first advent and will close with the return of the Lord to catch his bride—the church—away to heaven. Therefore, the entire current age, commonly known as the church age, is known as the last days.

Labeling this age as the "last days" is a vivid reminder that Christ could come at any time. Every generation since the death and resurrection of Christ has lived with the hope that it might be the final generation and that Christ could return at any moment. There are no prophecies that must be fulfilled before Christ can come. We are living in the last days and may be living in the last days of the last days before Christ's coming. As the end approaches, the enemy is ramping up the attacks in a final onslaught.

THE ULTIMATE SURVIVOR

Jesus, Paul, Peter, John, and others warn of an unprecedented increase in demonic deception, moral corruption, doctrinal error, and spiritual lethargy in the last days. Believers today face unparalleled spiritual danger. These are treacherous times. As Erwin Lutzer notes, "The day of the casual Christian is over. No longer is it possible to drift along, hoping that no tough choices will have to be made. At this point in American history, any moral and spiritual progress will have to be won at great cost. The darker the night, the more important every candle becomes."[2] We need to stand firm and shine brightly in the darkness.

In August 1990, Saddam Hussein invaded Kuwait, triggering the Gulf War. When she heard of the invasion, British Prime Minister Margaret Thatcher was in the United States. She described her initial thoughts in an interview with PBS's *Frontline*: "I went out for a walk, always lovely in the mountains, and got things worked out in my mind, but it was perfectly clear, aggression must be stopped. That is the lesson of this century. And if an aggressor gets away with it, others will want to get away with it too, so he must be stopped, and turned back. You cannot gain from your aggression."[3]

Toward the end of her tenure as prime minister, Thatcher helped spur President George H. W. Bush to intervene militarily in the Persian Gulf after the Iraqi invasion. Urging President Bush to join the fight against Saddam, Thatcher famously declared that "this is no time to go wobbly."[4] The same is true for us—this is no time to go wobbly.

But how can we stand strong in perilous times? How can we shine brightly in the darkness? How can we keep from "going wobbly" as the end of the age draws near?

GIVE ME THE TOOLS

Winston Churchill was prime minister of Great Britain during the trying days of World War II. Despite his massive influence, he often downplayed his own part in winning the war. He gave credit to the people, saying after the war had ended that they "had the lion's heart," and he merely "had the luck to be called upon to give the roar." In February 1941, Churchill delivered one of his most lauded wartime speeches. He claimed that in wartime, what mattered was "deeds, not words." After walking listeners through what had already transpired in the war, he urged US President Franklin Roosevelt to get involved in the fight rather than sitting on the sidelines. He said, "We shall not fail or falter; we shall not weaken or tire. Neither the sudden shock of battle, nor the long-drawn trials of vigilance and exertion will wear us down. Give us the tools, and we will finish the job."[5]

There's no doubt the church of Jesus Christ is locked in a deadly spiritual war. Sitting on the sidelines is not an option. The war is multiplying on numerous fronts. The good news is that God has given us the tools, or maybe it would be better to call them the truths, that we need to finish the job as we await Christ's coming. God has given us sufficient resources to effectively encounter and engage the world we're facing.

Many have wondered in recent years why the apocalypse craze in movies and video games appeals to people so strongly. One answer is "because they show people returning to the fundamentals of existence."[6] In the same way, I believe what's happening in our world today is moving believers to return to the foundations of our spiritual existence. Believers everywhere must get back to what matters most. We must always remember that our battle "at the most basic level is spiritual, not political or even moral."[7]

Some Christians today are carefully preparing *physically* for the apocalypse—hoarding cash, gold, weapons, and food. To one degree or another they're the ultimate "doomsday preppers."[8] There's nothing wrong with reasonable preparation for disruptions in basic services that could occur in our complex world; however, the most important "prepping" for every believer should be *spiritual*. Whatever view we may hold concerning the apocalypse or the end times, our focus should be on spiritual survival. That's the consistent focus of Scripture.

So, what are the spiritual tools, the spiritual truths, Scripture tells us we must understand and use as the end draws near? How can we be spiritually prepared for today and for what lies ahead?

In the pages that follow, you will discover ten spiritual tools the Bible relates directly to our spiritual preparation for the Lord's coming—ten biblical survival strategies to live out these last days so you and your family can prosper in an increasingly decaying, darkening world.

These strategies won't guarantee your physical or financial well-being, but they are guaranteed to bring life and vitality to your spiritual health and welfare as you cling to the immovable rock of God's Word. The truth is that even if you survive physically and prosper financially, your deepest need—and mine—is spiritual survival and stability. When life is whittled down to its essence, the real issue is our spiritual condition before God.

My prayer is that God can use these basic, biblical tools and strategies to help you survive and thrive as you await Christ's coming.

Mark Hitchcock
JANUARY 2018

CHAPTER I

USE THE 46 DEFENSE

Most news . . . could carry a universal headline to get our attention:
YOU SHOULD BE WORRIED.

GARY STOKES

ONE OF THE GREATEST DEFENSES in NFL history was that of the 1985 Chicago Bears. They employed a defensive scheme known as the "46 defense," developed in 1981 by defensive coordinator Buddy Ryan. Armed with this scheme and some great talent, they throttled and terrorized offenses across the league, reaching their zenith in 1985. The pressure they applied, led by middle linebacker Mike Singletary, was reckless and relentless. The '85 Bears struck fear into the hearts of opposing quarterbacks, blazing a trail of devastation through the NFL. Their domination was so overwhelming that "during one three-game stretch, the Bears scored more points on defense than they allowed, and they're the only team in history to post back-to-back shutouts in the playoffs."[1]

THE END TIMES SURVIVAL GUIDE

The 46 defense is legendary. None has ever been better.

As our world becomes more volatile and uncertain, wouldn't it be nice to have that kind of spiritual defense against the mounting cares, stresses, and worries of life? Wouldn't it be comforting to have an impenetrable wall that holds back the fear and fretting that floods our minds with anxious thoughts?

The truth is that God *has* given his people a "46 defense" against the cares, worries, and anxieties we face. It's a 46 defense that's better known even than that of the '85 Bears. It's Philippians 4:6. (We'll look at another famous 46 defense—Psalm 46—in chapter 7.)

The "Philippians 4:6" defense is renowned. It shuts down opposing offenses. They have no chance against it. It's a fail-safe formula against worry and stress:

> Don't worry about anything; instead, pray about everything. Tell God what you need, and thank him for all he has done. Then you will experience God's peace, which exceeds anything we can understand. His peace will guard your hearts and minds as you live in Christ Jesus.
>
> PHILIPPIANS 4:6-7

In anxious times, with worry on the offensive, more and more people are using it. Amazon tracks information about the most highlighted passages in their e-books. This list of what people highlight or annotate sheds light on what people find interesting, important, or valuable. According to Amazon, the verse in the Bible that is most frequently highlighted is not a traditionally familiar one like Psalm 23, John 3:16, or the Lord's Prayer—it is Philippians 4:6-7.[2] Apparently, it has become "America's go-to passage of Scripture."[3]

This shouldn't surprise us, because by all accounts, the United States is the most anxious nation in the world. Ironically, one of the world's wealthiest nations is also the most worried.

We live in a world of cascading crises. The world and its troubles and trials seem to be getting worse.

Jesus told us this would happen. In his famous sermon about the end times, just a few days before his death, Jesus outlined the signs of his coming and concluded by warning about the worries of life that can overwhelm us. Jesus said, "Watch out! Don't let your hearts be dulled by carousing and drunkenness, and by *the worries of this life*. Don't let that day catch you unaware, like a trap. For that day will come upon everyone living on the earth" (Luke 21:34-35, emphasis added).

Jesus said that the "worries of this life" in the final days will get so strong and will dull our hearts to such an extent that we might lose our hope and expectation of his coming if we allow them to go unchecked.

The worries of this life produce anxious days and sleepless nights. They distract us. They threaten our spiritual survival in these last days. Jesus said they're traps that dull our hearts and leave us unprepared for his coming. We can't thrive spiritually at the same time our hearts are weighed down with worry. But let's face it: maybe only a few of us worry none of the time, most of us worry some of the time, and some of us worry all the time.

Worry is a national addiction. You could even call it a plague. "Anxiety has become the number one mental health issue in North America. It's estimated that one third of the North American adult population experiences anxiety unwellness issues."[4]

Part of the explanation for the surge of worry is our constant connection to everything that's going on all over the world. Through 24-7 cable news, the Internet, and smartphones, we instantly know about nuclear threats, child kidnappings, famines, disasters, riots, economic problems, and on and on and on. The daily load of bad news can overwhelm us. Before means of mass communication, people lived mostly secluded lives. News traveled slowly, and sometimes not at all. How things have changed. Immediate access to world news threatens to crush us with stress and worry.

When Jesus spoke of the end times and the worries of this life, he knew that these worries would grow to the point that people are paralyzed and trapped. We all sense that anxiety is increasing and intensifying as the end draws near. We're anxious about all kinds of things:

> World problems and politics
> Our health
> Our finances and the economy
> Our children or grandchildren

> Our marriages
> Our choices
> Retirement
> Death
> What has happened
> What could happen

Sometimes we even get worried that we don't have anything to worry about.

We hear more and more about anxiety attacks, panic attacks, and people just generally being stressed out. Anti-anxiety drugs regularly appear on the top ten list of prescription medications in the United States. Many people have turned worry into a lifestyle, a full-time job. Life is consumed with worry and fear.

This reminds me of a story I heard about a woman who for many years had trouble sleeping because she worried about burglars. One night her husband heard a noise in the house, so he went downstairs to investigate. When he got there, he found a burglar and said, "I'm pleased to see you. Will you please come upstairs? My wife has been waiting ten years to meet you."

It's far too easy for worry to become a way of life and for us even to find ourselves worrying about the same things for years. But for God's people, life shouldn't be that way. A real burglar can steal from you once, but worry can steal from you night after night for years.

As the stresses of life multiply in these last days, how can we win over worry? How can we bury worry before worry buries us? What's the spiritual survival strategy?

We have to employ the Philippians 4:6 defense.

And this defense is strikingly simple. The antidote to anxiety is thankful prayer. To state it more fully: *we experience God's peace instead of worry when we pray with thankfulness.*

We can't worry and pray at the same time.

The three simple parts of this strategy come from the three key words in this passage.

> The Problem: Worry
> The Prescription: Prayer
> The Promise: Peace

THE PROBLEM: WORRY

Philippians 4:6 begins with four sweeping words: "Don't worry about anything," or as some translations say, "Be anxious for nothing."

It doesn't say,

> "Be anxious for less"
> "Be anxious for a few things"
> "Be anxious for only one hour a day"
> "Be anxious for only the big things"

It says, "Be anxious for *nothing*." "Don't worry about *anything*." It's categorical. God's people are never to worry—period. About anything.

The word *worry* in the original Greek (*merimnao*) literally means "to be divided into parts." To worry or be anxious is to have a distracted, divided mind—a mind torn down the middle and pulled in different directions. The worried mind is restless, filled with tension, and unsettled, like a flag twisting in the wind. It's a mind fighting on two fronts. The English word *worry* comes from an old English word that means "to strangle." This is a fitting image, because we all know how worry strangles and squeezes the peace and enjoyment out of life. Sometimes anxiety can get to the point that the worrier actually feels short of breath.

Worrying is having your mind torn between the real and the possible. Worry feeds on the what-ifs of life. It's a stream of thoughts focused on fear of what might happen. I once heard someone say that worry pulls tomorrow's cloud over today's sunshine. The worrier lives in the past and the future, spending life crucified between two thieves that rob the present of its joy and vitality. Helmut Thielicke aptly describes worry as "*wandering in times not our own.*"

Anxiety Attacked

Jesus confronted worry in his Sermon on the Mount in Matthew 5–7. Interestingly, one-seventh of Jesus' famous sermon is about worry. That's fascinating and instructive. Here is the Master's wisdom on worry:

> That is why I tell you not to worry about everyday life—whether you have enough food and drink, or

enough clothes to wear. Isn't life more than food, and your body more than clothing? Look at the birds. They don't plant or harvest or store food in barns, for your heavenly Father feeds them. And aren't you far more valuable to him than they are? Can all your worries add a single moment to your life?

And why worry about your clothing? Look at the lilies of the field and how they grow. They don't work or make their clothing, yet Solomon in all his glory was not dressed as beautifully as they are. And if God cares so wonderfully for wildflowers that are here today and thrown into the fire tomorrow, he will certainly care for you. Why do you have so little faith?

So don't worry about these things, saying, "What will we eat? What will we drink? What will we wear?" These things dominate the thoughts of unbelievers, but your heavenly Father already knows all your needs. Seek the Kingdom of God above all else, and live righteously, and he will give you everything you need.

So don't worry about tomorrow, for tomorrow will bring its own worries. Today's trouble is enough for today.

MATTHEW 6:25-34

There's a lot here to unpack, but we'll just look at this passage briefly. Jesus uses the word *worry* five times (verses 25, 27, 28, 31, 34). He tells us three simple things about worry. First, worry is *fruitless*. It doesn't do any good. As Jesus said, "Can all your worries add a single moment to your life?" We see the worthlessness of worry in that most of the things we worry about never happen. We expend countless hours exhausting our emotions on events that never materialize.

Sometimes people will say or think something like "I know worry works because when I worry about something, it doesn't happen." But that doesn't mean the worry worked. It simply proves that most things we worry about never happen. Like Vance Havner once said, "Worry is like sitting in a rocking chair. It will give you something to do, but it won't get you anywhere." It doesn't produce a thing. Fretting is a lot of work for nothing.

A recent study discovered that "85 percent of what subjects worried about never happened, and with the 15 percent that did happen, 79 percent of subjects discovered either they could handle the difficulty better than expected, or the difficulty taught them a lesson worth learning. This means that 97 percent of what you worry over is not much more than a fearful mind punishing you with exaggerations and misperceptions."[5]

Worry doesn't do any good—and results in a great deal of bad.

Second, worry is *faithless*. Jesus put his finger on the core issue when he said, "Why do you have so little faith?" Worry brings our weak faith to the surface. Many of us believe God can take care of the "Sweet By and By," but we have trouble trusting him with the "Nasty Now and Now." We trust him for heaven but not for earth.

Worry is the opposite of trust. It's a failure to trust God to take care of us. Worry has been described as the stepchild of unbelief. We can dress it up and disguise it however we want to, but worry is nothing but lack of trust in God to meet our needs in his perfect time.

Third, Jesus says worry is *fatherless*. When we worry, we act as if we have no Father who cares for our needs and yearns to meet them. Jesus says, "Your heavenly Father already knows all your needs." Worry diminishes our heavenly Father's loving care for us. Think of how our worry must make God feel. When he sees us worried and afraid, we aren't trusting him. He is our Father, but we choose to live like we're orphans when we worry and fret.

We live under the canopy of God's fatherly care. In Matthew 6:26-30, there's an argument from the lesser to the greater. God loves his children more than his pets. If God cares for birds, he will care for us.

We are his children through faith in Jesus Christ. God is our Father—and he's a *perfect* father. We can trust him to care for us at all times, even during these dark days.

Worry Weary

With worry comes a host of unwanted results. Robert J. Morgan vividly outlines some of the consequences of an anxious outlook: "When worry barges into our brains, it brings along a gang of accomplices—discouragement, fear, exhaustion, despair, anguish, hopelessness, pain, obsession, distraction, foreboding, irritation, impatience—none of which are friends of the Holy Spirit."[6]

Anxiety saps your strength, leaving you spent and stressed out. Worry slowly drains our strength and focus. As the old saying goes, "Worry doesn't empty tomorrow of its sorrows, but it empties today of its strength."

It's not wrong to think about the future and to make plans. The book of Proverbs tells us in various ways that planning is wise. I love to plan and think about the future. It's fine and even faithful to *think* about tomorrow, as long as we submit our plans to the Lord, but it's never right to *worry* about the future.

At one point during his presidency, the people around Abraham Lincoln were anxious about coming events. In response to their worries, Lincoln told this story:

> Many years ago, when I was a young lawyer, and
> Illinois was little settled, except on her southern
> border, I, with other lawyers, used to ride the circuit;
> journeying with the judge from county-seat to
> county-seat in quest of business. Once, after a long
> spell of pouring rain, which had flooded the whole
> country, transforming small creeks into rivers, we
> were often stopped by these swollen streams, which
> we with difficulty crossed. Still ahead of us was Fox
> River, larger than all the rest; and we could not
> help saying to each other, "If these streams give us

so much trouble, how shall we get over Fox River?"
Darkness fell before we had reached that stream; and
we all stopped at a log tavern, had our horses put
out, and resolved to pass the night. Here we were
right glad to fall in with the Methodist Presiding
Elder of the circuit, who rode it in all weather, knew
all its ways, and could tell us all about Fox River.
So we all gathered around him, and asked him if he
knew about the crossing of Fox River. "O yes," he
replied, "I know all about Fox River. I have crossed
it often, and understand it well; but I have one fixed
rule with regard to Fox River: I never cross it till I
reach it."[7]

Far too many believers are wearing themselves out crossing the Fox River long before they reach it. Wait until you
get there.

Good Worry?

The Bible makes an important distinction between what we
might call "good worry" and "bad worry."

Philippians 4:6 says, "Don't worry about anything." Clearly
this is sinful worry. But in Philippians 2:20, the apostle Paul
lauds his friend Timothy when he says, "I have no one else
like Timothy, who genuinely cares about your welfare." The
phrase "genuinely cares" translates the same Greek word used
for "worry" in Philippians 4:6. So there is a kind of care that's

applauded and appropriate that we could call "concern" and another inappropriate form we could call "anxiety."

There are many good things to be concerned about. Our marriages. Our children. Our aged parents. Our own spiritual lives. The spiritual condition of our family and friends. The future and welfare of our nation. We all have genuine, legitimate concerns. There are many good things that should burden us—things we should care about. But genuine concern can quickly degenerate into godless worry or what Jesus called the "worries of this life."

We all know what it feels like to be concerned about something and suddenly feel our mind being pulled in different directions. Our thoughts become restless and distracted, and sleep evades us. We're tense and unsettled and feel like we're being pulled apart. We can feel the surge of uneasiness. We're moving from concern to worry—from "good" worry to "godless" worry.

The Bible is clear that we aren't to worry about anything. But how do we shake the worries of life?

THE PRESCRIPTION: PRAYER

In Philippians 4:6, the word "instead" (or "but" in some translations) appears right after the words "Don't worry about anything," drawing a sharp contrast. After the word "instead" we have God's prescription for worry: "Pray about everything. Tell God what you need, and thank him for all he has done." The antidote to anxiety is to pray about everything.

Three different Greek words for "prayer" are found in this verse. The first one is a general word for prayer in which we give adoration, worship, and devotion to God. The second term focuses on our needs and connotes the idea of dependence or a desperate cry arising from need. The third word refers to precise petitions or specific requests.

Jesus highlighted prayer as the antidote to anxiety in his sermon about the end times:

> Watch out! Don't let your hearts be dulled by
> carousing and drunkenness, and by the *worries of*
> *this life*. Don't let that day catch you unaware, like
> a trap. For that day will come upon everyone living
> on the earth. Keep alert at all times. And *pray* that
> you might be strong enough to escape these coming
> horrors and stand before the Son of Man.
>
> LUKE 21:34-36, EMPHASIS ADDED

Jesus says prayer is our defense against the worries of life. Robert J. Morgan vividly highlights the connection between prayer and overcoming the trap of worry:

> Prayer is the closet where we change clothes and
> replace a spirit of despair with a garment of praise.
> It's the bank where we present the promissory notes
> of God's promises and withdraw endless deposits of
> grace. It's the darkroom of the soul where negatives
> become positives. It's the transfer station where the

pulse of fear is exchanged for the impulse of faith. It's a currency exchange where we trade in our liabilities for God's abundant life.[8]

Prayer is our defense against the worries of life, but not just any prayer—*thankful* prayer. Philippians 4:6 includes the all-important words "and thank him for all he has done." Recalling God's blessings must accompany our prayers. When we give thanks, we're recognizing and remembering God's good gifts to us. This intentional recounting of God's blessings creates faith and trust. Grateful prayer builds our faith, pushing worry out of our hearts. Praying with an attitude of gratitude wipes out worry. Thankful prayer is the fail-safe formula that transfers our cares to God and taps into his peace.

As Charles Spurgeon once said, "No care but all prayer. No anxiety but much joyful communion with God. Carry your desires to the Lord of your life, the guardian of your soul. Go to Him with two portions of prayer and one of fragrant praise. Do not pray doubtfully but thankfully."[9]

As we plunge deeper into the end times, the worries of life will increase and intensify. We see it already. To survive and stand, we must run the 46 defense every day, every moment in our lives. You may have to use the 46 defense over and over again every day as worry tries to worm its way into your heart and mind. Every time worry knocks, immediately use the 46 defense. It will work every time.

THE PROMISE: PEACE

Few promises in the Bible are more comforting than Philippians 4:7: "Then you will experience God's peace, which exceeds anything we can understand. His peace will guard your hearts and minds as you live in Christ Jesus."

Did you catch those words? "God's peace." This is stunning. When a believer humbly approaches the throne of God in thankful prayer, the serenity of the Trinity is unleashed in that believer's heart. God has never experienced one worried moment. Nothing disturbs him. He's never shaken. He's perpetually at peace. There's never panic in heaven. The Trinity never meets in emergency session. God has an infinite, measureless supply of peace, and he makes that peace available to us by means of prayer.

There are two beautiful things in Philippians 4:7 about God's peace. First, it's *unexplainable*. The peace of God infinitely surpasses the ability of the human mind to perceive or understand how it works. It "defies all attempts to describe, analyze, explain, or comprehend it."[10] Charles Spurgeon says, "This shall bring you God's own peace. You shall not be able to understand the peace which you shall enjoy. It will enfold you in its infinite embrace. Heart and mind through Christ Jesus shall be steeped in a sea of rest. Come life or death, poverty, pain, slander, you shall dwell in Jesus above every rolling wind or darkening cloud."[11] I hope you've experienced this peace.

Our first son, Justin, was born while Cheryl and I lived in Dallas during my first semester at Dallas Theological

Seminary. Cheryl was in the hospital for a month before he was born. He was born very prematurely and had a cleft lip and palate. He spent his first six weeks in the neonatal intensive care unit at Baylor Hospital. During those dark days, I used the 46 defense over and over again. Every time, my cries to God were met with his supernatural calm. I still can't explain it. God's peace is unexplainable.

Second, the peace of God is *unassailable*. The word "guard" is a military term for a contingent of soldiers assigned to protect someone. The peace of God acts as a guard at the door of your heart and mind to provide security against the assaults of worry, confusion, tension, and uncertainty.

At the time Paul wrote the epistle to the Philippians, he was eight hundred miles away from them in Rome under house arrest, guarded 24-7 by the Roman Praetorian Guard, the most elite force in the Roman Empire. But as Steven J. Lawson points out, "He was also being guarded in a far more secure way—God was protecting his heart so that anxiety and fear would not enter it. Fear was being denied entrance into his heart. . . . anxiety cannot crack the divine defense."[12] The believer who prays with thanksgiving is guarded against the assault of anxiety.

As we're hurtling toward the end of days and the worries-of-life mushroom, God's peace is like a spiritual "SEAL Team Six" stationed at the entrance of your thoughts and emotions to protect and keep you, giving you mental and emotional stability and tranquility.

Philippians 4:7 ends with the comforting words "in

Christ Jesus." In Jesus we have nothing to fear; without him we have everything to fear. Jesus is our peace.

Joseph Scriven said it well in the hymn "What a Friend We Have in Jesus":

What a friend we have in Jesus,
all our sins and griefs to bear!
What a privilege to carry
everything to God in prayer!
O what peace we often forfeit,
O what needless pain we bear,
all because we do not carry
everything to God in prayer.

Don't forfeit God's peace. Don't go on bearing needless pain. Carry everything to God in grateful prayer. Use the 46 defense. Claim God's fathomless, unshakable peace.

NO WORRIES

An early Greek manuscript bears the name of a man called Titedios Amerimnos. The first name is a proper name—like the name Titus. The second name is like a nickname, and it is made up of the word that means "to worry" (*merimnos*) prefixed by the Greek letter alpha, which negates the meaning of the word. *Amerimnos* means "not to worry." Based on this nickname, many believe this man was a Greek who constantly worried but who stopped worrying once he was saved.

Thereafter he was known as Titedios Amerimnos—"Titedio, the man who never worries."[13]

The question for us is, can we write our name and add to it, "The One Who Never Worries"? This will only be true if we learn the spiritual survival strategy of thankful prayer.

We must use the prescription in Philippians 4:6 and claim the promise in Philippians 4:7. There's no need to have any more anxious days and sleepless nights.

Some days and nights you may have to use the 46 defense over and over again. You may have to go to the Lord in thankful prayer again and again. But you can rest assured it will work every time. God's perpetual peace is available if we will humbly lift our hearts to him in grateful prayer. The only question is, will we obey this clear command? If we will, our days and nights of worry are over.

In my early twenties I spent two to three hours every Friday night studying the Bible with an elderly friend. He was a faithful, loving Bible teacher who helped me a great deal. He had several adages he liked to repeat, but there was one saying he repeated most often—"When in a fix, go to Philippians 4:6." I know it's a bit corny, but I've never forgotten it. I still apply it often today. I hope you will too.

"When in a fix, go to Philippians 4:6."

This world is not becoming a safer, more stable, or more secure place. As technology explodes and threats expand, the potential for worry widens. Stress surges. Jesus lovingly warned us about the prevalence and peril of the "worries of this life" that threaten our spiritual strength, stamina, and stability as this age draws to a close, and through the pen of the apostle Paul, he graciously gave us a fail-safe defense that will work every time—the 46 defense:

> Don't worry about anything; instead, pray about everything. Tell God what you need, and thank him for all he has done. Then you will experience God's peace, which exceeds anything we can understand. His peace will guard your hearts and minds as you live in Christ Jesus.

CHAPTER 2

RUN FOR YOUR LIFE

We ain't gonna have no sport where you sit down and go backwards.

CLEMSON ATHLETIC DIRECTOR FRANK HOWARD,

IN RESPONSE TO A SUGGESTION THAT CLEMSON FIELD

A ROWING TEAM

IN A DEVOTION TITLED "Run for Your Life," Philip De Courcy references Christopher McDougall's *Born to Run*: "Every morning in Africa, a gazelle wakes up, it knows it must outrun the fastest lion or it will be killed. Every morning in Africa, a lion wakes up, it knows it must run faster than the slowest gazelle, or it will starve. It doesn't matter whether you're the lion or the gazelle, when the sun comes up, you'd better be running."[1]

De Courcy writes, "Not to do something is to have something done to you. If the gazelle fails to run it gets eaten, if the lion fails to run it has nothing to eat. Both the gazelle and lion must run for their life. And so it is with the Christian."[2]

When I look around today, I believe more strongly than ever that the end of days is near. On every front, world events bear a remarkable correspondence to ancient prophecies in

Scripture. As time runs out, we need to run as never before—we need to run for our lives. Our enemy, Satan, is on the prowl. He knows his time is short. The "lion" wakes up every day and never stops roaming, searching for prey (see 1 Peter 5:8). Standing still is not an option. If you stand still, you'll get swallowed up. We must run and keep running, which requires spiritual stamina and endurance.

The disappointments and discouragements of life can sap our strength and will. And underneath the bigger struggles of life is the daily grind and routine that can slowly wear us down. As I once heard someone say, "The problem with life is that it's so daily." We need to run with endurance.

Christians should not be strangers to running. Athletic metaphors are liberally sprinkled throughout the New Testament, especially in the writings of the apostle Paul, who must have witnessed the games many times in his day. He often compares the Christian life to a race.

> Don't you realize that in a race everyone runs, but only one person gets the prize? So run to win! All athletes are disciplined in their training. They do it to win a prize that will fade away, but we do it for an eternal prize. So I run with purpose in every step. I am not just shadowboxing. I discipline my body like an athlete, training it to do what it should. Otherwise, I fear that after preaching to others I myself might be disqualified.
>
> I CORINTHIANS 9:24-27

I don't mean to say that I have already achieved these things or that I have already reached perfection. But I press on to possess that perfection for which Christ Jesus first possessed me. No, dear brothers and sisters, I have not achieved it, but I focus on this one thing: Forgetting the past and looking forward to what lies ahead, I press on to reach the end of the race and receive the heavenly prize for which God, through Christ Jesus, is calling us.

PHILIPPIANS 3:12-14

I have fought the good fight, I have finished the race, and I have remained faithful. And now the prize awaits me—the crown of righteousness, which the Lord, the righteous Judge, will give me on the day of his return. And the prize is not just for me but for all who eagerly look forward to his appearing.

2 TIMOTHY 4:7-8

Hebrews 12:1-2 is the key New Testament text on how to run the race of life with focus and endurance—on how to run for your life:

Therefore, since we are surrounded by such a huge crowd of witnesses to the life of faith, let us strip off every weight that slows us down, especially the sin that so easily trips us up. And let us run with endurance the race God has set before us. We do this by keeping our eyes on Jesus, the champion who initiates and perfects our faith. Because of the joy awaiting him, he endured the cross, disregarding its shame. Now he is seated in the place of honor beside God's throne.

William Barclay, the well-known biblical commentator, calls these two verses "a well-nigh perfect summary of the Christian life."[3] These verses picture the Christian race from the starting blocks to the finish line. They fall neatly into six parts.

THE EXHORTATION

The key statement in Hebrews 12:1-2 is "and let us run with endurance the race God has set before us." Everything around this statement in Hebrews 12:1-2 describes how we run our race with endurance. But before we unpack this statement, let's get our bearings within the book of Hebrews. This anonymous epistle was penned in the early AD 60s for believers residing in the city of Rome, likely before the outbreak of Nero's persecution. The litany of Old Testament quotations and allusions point toward Jewish Christians ("Hebrews") as the primary audience. The readers have trusted Jesus as their Messiah and are now suffering mistreatment from both Gentiles and Jews. Hebrews 10:32-36 describes their situation and the author's call to hang in there:

Think back on those early days when you first learned about Christ. Remember how you remained faithful even though it meant terrible suffering. Sometimes you were exposed to public ridicule and were beaten, and sometimes you helped others who were suffering the same things. You suffered along with those who were thrown into jail, and when all you owned was taken from you, you accepted it with joy. You knew there were better things waiting for you that will last forever. So do not throw away this confident trust in the Lord. Remember the great reward it brings you! Patient endurance is what you need now, so that you will continue to do God's will. Then you will receive all that he has promised.

The troubles have reached the point where some of the believers are tempted to jettison Jesus and revert to their old way of life. They're in danger of flaming out and fizzling out.

Many believe the book of Hebrews was originally a sermon to stir the audience to keep going. The dominant theme of the letter is the supremacy of Jesus. The first three verses set the tone:

Long ago God spoke many times and in many ways to our ancestors through the prophets. And now in these final days, he has spoken to us through his Son. God promised everything to the Son as an inheritance, and through the Son he created the universe. The Son radiates God's own glory and expresses the very character of God, and he sustains

everything by the mighty power of his command.
When he had cleansed us from our sins, he sat
down in the place of honor at the right hand of the
majestic God in heaven.

After this grand opening, chapters 1 through 10 show that Jesus is greater than angels, greater than Moses, greater than Aaron, and greater than Old Testament sacrifices. The message is to stay focused on Jesus. He is supreme—why on earth would readers want to leave him and go back to their old way of life?

Within this larger context, Hebrews 12:1-2 is like a dose of spiritual smelling salts to help these believers, and us, get a second wind in the race. It's a call for us to run for our lives in the face of increasing opposition and buffeting spiritual headwinds.

The word "race" in Hebrews 12:1 is the Greek word *agona* (from which we get our English word *agony*). Anyone who has ever run any significant distance knows that running a long way involves a degree of agony and exhaustion.

Years ago, while visiting my in-laws in Dallas for Thanksgiving, my wife talked me into running an eight-mile race called the Turkey Trot on Thanksgiving morning. I was running about three miles a day back then and thought a few more miles would be no problem, so off we went. I was right to a point. I felt great for the first three miles. And the next two or three weren't bad either (the first five or six miles were fairly flat). But the last two or three miles were grueling. All the hills were in the final stretch. The finish line in the distance was one of the most welcome sights I've ever seen. I finished the race, but I vowed never to do that again. Since then, I've always wondered why people like to run long distances.

I sympathize with Joe Stowell's attitude toward running:

I have nothing against runners. Some of my best friends are addicted runners. Though I have never seen a runner smiling, apparently there is something fulfilling about it. I even tried it once, waiting for that surge of ecstasy that my friends told me I would experience, only to find that the ecstasy came when I stopped running.[4]

Stowell continues:

Whatever you think about running, it's important to note that the Bible often speaks of living the Christian life as if . . . we were running a race. Following Jesus is clearly more than a leisurely stroll in the park! And the issue is not whether you will run the race. When you became His follower, you were put in the race. The question is not *will* you run, but *how* will you run?[5]

We're called to run the race of life with endurance. And we each have our own race to run. Hebrews 12:1 calls this "the race marked out for us" (NIV). We each have a lane to run in. Our Lord has mapped out a specific race for each of us. Our races vary greatly. No two races are the same. We each face our own set of challenges. As Kent Hughes reminds us,

> We each have a specific course mapped out for us, and the course for each runner is unique. Some are relatively straight, some are all turns, some seem all uphill, some are a flat hiking path. All are long, but some are longer. But each of us . . . can finish the race "marked out for us." I may not be able to run your course, and you may find mine impossible, but I can finish my race and you yours. Both of us can finish well if we choose and if we rely on him who is our strength and our guide.[6]

That's the exhortation.

THE ENCOURAGEMENT

The exhortation to run the race is preceded by a wonderful encouragement: "Therefore, since we are surrounded by such a huge crowd of witnesses." We all desperately need encouragement in the race. The word "therefore" that opens Hebrews 12:1 is a transition word that reaches back to the long list of the faithful in Hebrews 11. The "huge crowd of witnesses" pictures a capacity crowd at a stadium. Few things are more electrifying than a stadium full of loyal fans. There's nothing that can match the wave of enthusiasm that sweeps over a packed college football stadium on a Saturday afternoon in the fall.

Many understand this to mean that all the saints who lived before us are spectators in a great stadium in heaven, watching us and cheering us on. But the picture here is not of *them* watching *us* but of *us* watching *them*. In other words, they testify to us and bear witness to us that God can see us through. When we look at the lives of men and women like Enoch, Abraham, Sarah, Jacob, Rahab, David, and Daniel, we are encouraged. They all faced struggles, tests of faith, and temptation, yet they finished the race. They didn't quit. They didn't go back. That's the point the author of Hebrews is driving home. The lives of these Old Testament saints are a motivation and incentive for the original readers and for us not to go back. That's why we need to study the lives of the saints of old. They stayed in the race and finished; so can we.

The *exhortation* is clear: run with endurance.

The *encouragement* is comforting: look to the witnesses.

But there's another thing every runner must do to win: eliminate the encumbrances and the entanglements.

THE ENCUMBRANCES

Here we move from the stands down to the track as the runners are preparing to run, getting ready for the race: "Let us strip off every weight that slows us down." The first thing any runner does is to work to eliminate drag.

The Greek word translated here as "weight" (*ogkos*) is the

word from which we get our English word *oncology*, and it refers to a mass, tumor, or weight. Runners do all they can to shed excess body weight. You never see a chubby marathon runner—at least not one who is competitive. They also peel off any shred of excess clothing. You will never see a competitive runner on race day wearing sweatpants or ankle weights.

In the same way, as we run our race, we must throw off everything that holds us back. Anything that slows our progress must go.

These encumbrances in our lives aren't sinful things. They're things that distract and delay us, that sap our energy, that divert our attention, and that dampen our enthusiasm for the things of God. They're anything that dulls our competitive edge. We know they're not sinful things because they're distinguished from sins in the next phrase ("the sin that so easily trips us up"). This tells us that just because something is not a sin doesn't make it right for us. A good thing can become a bad thing if it slows us down or impedes our progress.

What are the encumbrances that can weigh us down? Some examples could be too much recreation and entertainment, our careers, our habits, our hobbies, sports, relationships, lack of discipline, or procrastination. Encumbrances vary from person to person.

We would all do well to search our hearts and ask, *What encumbrances are in my life? What am I doing to rid myself of them?*

THE ENTANGLEMENTS

The author of Hebrews moves seamlessly from "every weight that slows us down" to "the sin that so easily trips us up." These are bad things; they're sin. The use of the definite article, *the*, before the word *sin* could indicate that a specific sin is in view. In the context of the book of Hebrews, the main threat to the believers seems to have been a creeping unbelief (see Hebrews 3:12, 19). Hebrews 11 is all about faith, so in this context *the* sin could be a reference to un-belief (lack of faith) or doubt. After all, the phrase "by faith" occurs twenty-one times in Hebrews 11. The Lord may be warning us to put aside unbelief, which is a faucet for all kinds of other sins.

While that view is certainly possible, I think *the* sin referred to in Hebrews 12:1 is probably broader. We all face entangling, ensnaring sins in our lives. They are often referred to as "besetting" sins because the King James Version refers to this as "the sin which doth so easily beset us." We could call this "the sin which clings so closely." We each have certain sins that cling closely to us, although they're not the same for every person: pride, greed, lust, worry, gossip, laziness, jealousy, impatience, addiction, anger, self-pity, ingratitude, hatred, bitterness, unforgiveness, or a critical spirit. J. C. Ryle exposes our special sins:

> But there are particular besetting sins, of which each separate Christian can alone furnish an account; each single one of us has some weak point; each one has

got a thin, shaking spot in the wall of defence against the devil, each one has a traitor in his camp ready to open the gates to Satan, and he that is wise will never rest until he has discovered where this weak point is. This is that special sin which you are here exhorted to watch against, to overcome, to cast forth, to spare no means in keeping it under and bringing it into subjection, that it may not entangle you in the race towards Zion. One man is beset with lust, another with a love of drinking, another with an evil temper, another with malice, another with covetousness, another with worldly-mindedness, another with idleness; but each of us has got about him some besetting infirmity, which is able to hinder him far more than others, and with which he must keep an unceasing warfare, or else he will never so run as to obtain the prize.[7]

As the storm clouds gather and the world grows darker, the encumbrances and entanglements are increasing. Sin is nothing new, but its manifestations seem to be proliferating before our eyes. More and more our world mirrors the days of Noah, when "everything they thought or imagined was consistently and totally evil" (Genesis 6:5). Os Guinness laments, "Evil in the advanced modern world flaunts itself under the cover of the cool, the global, the connected and the accessible. . . . This magnification of evil is profound."[8]

Do you know what your entangling sin or sins are? Are

you brutally honest and self-aware, or do you hide and make excuses for yourself? Do you seek the Lord about them? Do you pray for his help and strength? Are you serious about guarding your life from them? Do you avail yourself of the means of grace—Scripture, prayer, fellowship, confession, and service? To run effectively and efficiently, we have to get rid of the encumbrances and entanglements.

THE EXAMPLE

Next the author of Hebrews points us to the example: "We do this by keeping our eyes on Jesus, the champion who initiates and perfects our faith." In every ancient Roman arena there was an emperor's box. Every competitor would look to see if the emperor was in attendance on the day of his race and was watching. When we look for our emperor, he's there. And Jesus is not only watching us, he's out ahead of us all the way. He's been through the race himself. He has blazed the trail for us and completed the course. He endured to the point of bearing the cross and its shame.

He's called the "champion who initiates . . . our faith," which means he's our pioneer or leader. He is the embodiment of trust in God—the preeminent example and model of faith. We draw some great encouragement from the lives of the faithful saints in Hebrews 11 who've gone before us, but the consummate example for us to follow is Jesus. We look to him. He is our pursuit and our prize.

Yet far too many believers have their gaze directed on the past—past sins, past sorrows, and past successes. Looking back will paralyze your progress. The apostle Paul had a laser-like forward focus: "I focus on this one thing: Forgetting the past and looking forward to what lies ahead, I press on to reach the end of the race and receive the heavenly prize" (Philippians 3:13-14). "Forgetting" doesn't mean you don't remember the past, but it carries the idea of not being influenced by it. You can't drive a car by looking in the rearview mirror or the back-up camera—at least not very far or very well. You can't run a race if you're looking back over your shoulder.

There's an example of this memorialized in a bronze statue at Empire Fields in Vancouver. The British Empire and Commonwealth Games were held in the newly constructed Empire Stadium on August 7, 1954. Two competitors— England's Roger Bannister and Australian John Landy—had both run sub-four-minute miles earlier that year, breaking the records of the time. Bannister had accomplished this feat first, and then Landy beat the new record a month later. This was their first meeting, and a crowd of thirty-five thousand was present to watch what was hailed as "The Mile of the Century."

The race was close all the way, and then almost at the end of the race, Landy, who had the lead, looked over his left shoulder to see where Bannister was, which caused Landy momentarily to break stride. At that moment Bannister passed him on his right side and won the race. To this day it stands as one of the most dramatic moments in sports history and has become known as "the Miracle Mile," and the statue at Empire Fields captures Bannister passing Landy while his head was turned.

Looking back will break your stride. Don't be influenced by what's behind. Look ahead. Look to Jesus. He's our Example.

But Jesus isn't just our *Example*. He's our *Enabler*. He's the one who "perfects," finishes, or completes our faith. He's the *Pioneer* who shows the way, but he's also the *Power* that energizes us to make it to the finish line and win. We don't have to persevere in our own strength and willpower. Thank God for that.

THE END

Because of the joy awaiting him, he endured the cross, disregarding its shame. Now he is seated in the place of honor beside God's throne.

HEBREWS 12:2

Endurance requires anticipation and motivation. That's why all races end with reward. The final point of every race is the finish line, followed by the awarding of prizes for those who finished well. No one runs a race without the expectation of reward if they win. This was true of the games in ancient Greece and Rome.

The apostle Paul, near the end of his life, looked toward the goal when he said, "I press on to reach the end of the race and receive the heavenly prize for which God, through Christ Jesus, is calling us" (Philippians 3:14).

Even Jesus endured life here on earth because of the reward at the end of the race. Jesus looked forward to the reward of his exaltation in glory—joy. In the same way, the anticipation of future reward fuels us to keep running.

When rewards are handed out, Max Lucado reminds us, "The small will be great. The forgotten will be remembered. The unnoticed will be crowned, and the faithful will be honored."[9] The Bible doesn't tell us all we would like to know about rewards in heaven, but Lucado boils it down fairly well: "While we're not sure exactly what those rewards are, we do know they include heavenly applause, God's approval, and eternal life. What else would you want?"[10]

KEEP ON

If we're going to survive spiritually in the troubled times that surround us, we'd better hit the ground running every morning. Standing still is a killer. We must run with endurance the particular race God has marked out for us, all the time remembering that—

> *Behind us* are the faithful saints spurring us on.
> *Around us* are encumbrances and entanglements we need to shed.
> *Before us* and *ahead of us* is Jesus, our Example and Enabler.
> *Awaiting us* are rewards.

Maybe you have never entered the race. Many today are trying to win a race they haven't entered. If you've never put your faith in Jesus Christ as Savior and Lord, you aren't even in the race. Hebrews 7:25 says, "Therefore He is able also to save forever those who draw near to God through Him" (NASB). God will save you forever if you come to him through his Son, Jesus. Don't delay. Come now. Get in the race.

Some of us are in the early race. If that's you, get serious. Set the pace early for your own life and for your family. Throw off the encumbrances and entanglements. It never gets easier to get rid of them than now. Disciplines practiced and perfected early in life will be a great benefit as you go farther in the race.

Some of us are in the middle of the race or a little beyond. At this point the race may seem like a slog. You may be hitting the wall. Fix your eyes on Jesus. Look to him to lead the way and give you strength.

Some may be approaching the finish line. Don't give up. Finish strong. Finishing is hard; finishing well is harder. We don't want to end before we finish, with days unredeemed. We want to end and finish at the same time—and finish well. It will be worth it.

Stay focused. Keep running. Don't give up, no matter how hard it gets and no matter how winded you may feel.

Dr. Eric Alexander, a renowned Scottish pastor, relates this story about the importance of persevering as we run the race to win:

> While I was still a theological student, Dr. Martyn Lloyd-Jones came from London to Glasgow to preach at the great St. Andrews Hall. . . . After the

meeting finished, I was waiting at the side of the platform for transport home. A long line of people were waiting to speak to Dr. Lloyd-Jones. . . . Interestingly, I noticed that every encounter ended in the same way: "Keep on!" was the doctor's final exhortation as he shook hands.

As it happened, on the journey home I was in the same car as the doctor, and he engaged me in conversation. After the generalities, I summoned enough courage to ask him a question. "Doctor," I began, "forgive me, but I could not help hearing your last words to every person you spoke with. They were 'Keep on.' It sounded as if that was particularly important to you." He was immediately animated: "My dear man," he said, "there is nothing more important. The Christian life is not a sprint; it is a marathon."[11]

Great words for each of us to live by—*keep on!*
Great words for us to say to one another often—*keep on!*
I believe we're getting near the end. All the signs point in that direction. We need to run like never before.
Keep on!
Run for your life.
The prize awaits you.

CHAPTER 3

MAKE A GOOD CONNECTION

The New Testament does not envisage solitary religion.

C. S. LEWIS

---

*Don't ever come to church without coming as though it were
the first time, as though it could be the best time and
as though it might be the last time.*

VANCE HAVNER

I LIKE THE STORY OF THE MOTHER who went to wake her son for church one Sunday morning. When she knocked on his door, he said, "I'm not going!"

"Why not?" asked his mother.

"I'll give you two good reasons," he said. "One, they don't like me. Two, I don't like them."

His mother replied, "I'll give you two good reasons why you *will* go to church. One, you're forty-seven years old. Two, you're the pastor!"

Scenes like this one are becoming common in churches today in America. More and more people seem to be AWOL on Sunday mornings. Increasingly, Sunday has become a day for sleeping in and going out, not turning up for worship.

Statistics bear out the decline in church attendance. One of the most startling aspects of the current trend is the movement of younger evangelicals away from the church. John S. Dickerson writes, "Research indicates that more than half of those born into evangelicalism are leaving the movement during their twenties. And the majority of them never return. This departure figure has never been higher in the United States. The number of those who return has never been lower."[1] Josh McDowell found that "69 percent of evangelical teens leave the church after high school."[2] LifeWay Research discovered that "70 percent of Christian church attendees from the millennial generation quit attending church by age twenty-three."[3] George Barna "estimates that from every five young evangelicals, four will 'disengage' from the church by age twenty-nine."[4]

While the most significant bleeding is coming from the millennial generation, the overall picture of church attendance and participation is not pretty. Thom Rainer puts his finger on what may be the number one reason church attendance is declining:

> Most of us have our own ideas why attendance is declining. Many have suggested that our nation is shifting away from its Christian roots, and thus the churches are declining as a smaller proportion of our country are believers in Christ. I certainly will not argue with that premise. Certainly attendance declines are related to massive cultural shifts in our

nation. But I would also suggest that one reason for declines has a greater impact than others. Stated simply, the number one reason for the decline in church attendance is that members attend with less frequency than they did just a few years ago. . . . No members left the church. Everyone is still relatively active in the church. But attendance declined over 12 percent because half the members changed their attendance behavior slightly.[5]

Ask most pastors, and they will confirm that members attend church less frequently than they did ten or twenty years ago. I've seen this in the church I pastor. To maintain the same attendance level requires more members because people come less often. The trend is troubling. Many more reasons for this phenomenon could be cited.

Donald Whitney suggests a few of the most common ones:

Ask why people don't attend church, and you'll get a variety of responses. . . . Some say they don't go to church because they are turned off by what seems an endless asking for money. Others stay away because church services bore them. A percentage of those who have no interest in church say the sermons are irrelevant to their lives. Some refuse to go because when they do attend they leave feeling guilty.

Numbers of people stay home because Sunday is their only day off and they want to spend it doing other things. . . .

A few stay away because they think their lifestyle is too unacceptable to the expectations of churchgoers. A lot of folks are convinced the church simply has nothing to offer them. . . . And one of the most common reasons given why people don't go to church is that there just isn't time.[6]

My main purpose in this chapter is not to diagnose why people don't attend church but to challenge you, in these last days, to find a church that faithfully preaches the gospel of Jesus Christ, loves people, and serves the church and the world, and to consistently show up, support the church financially, and connect with the people there. Why? Because God created us for relationship. We're hardwired for relationship with him and with others. We must have a relationship with God's Son, Jesus Christ, to have true life and salvation. After that, much of our growth as believers comes through the interaction and accountability that fellow believers supply within spiritual community. The Bible calls us to be with God's people regularly because the Lord knows our spiritual survival is at stake. Isolation is not God's will for his children. Isolation in today's environment is dangerous and spiritually deadly.

Filmmaker Alex Gibney directed a documentary titled *Steve Jobs: The Man in the Machine*. Summarizing the thrust of the documentary, one writer says, "What *The Man in the*

Machine really wants to present is the contradiction of Jobs's legacy: that he developed a technology that sought to connect while he lived a life of disconnection (alienating colleagues, pushing his girlfriend and daughter away, etc.)."[7] What an irony. The man who connected the world lived an isolated existence.

Jobs's story is far from unique. More and more people, including professing Christians, are settling for detached, disengaged lives and are reaping the consequences.

Challenging the millennial generation, Kevin DeYoung says,

> It's possible we talk a lot about authentic community but we aren't willing to live in it. The church is not an incidental part of God's plan. Jesus didn't invite people to join an anti-religion, anti-doctrine, anti-institutional bandwagon of love, harmony, and re-integration. He showed people how to live, to be sure. But He also called them to repent, called them to faith, called them out of the world, and called them into the church. The Lord "didn't add them to the church without saving them, and he didn't save them without adding them to the church" [quoting John Stott].[8]

DeYoung concludes with this wise warning: "Don't give up on the church. The New Testament knows nothing of churchless Christianity. The invisible church is for invisible

Christians. The visible church is for you and me. Put away the Che Guevara t-shirts, stop the revolution, and join the rest of the plodders. Fifty years from now you'll be glad you did."[9]

There are all kinds of ways to express the need we have as God's people to connect with others. Togetherness. Networking. Fellowship. Doing life together. But whatever you call it, we all need it. Clearly, not every person can be in church. Attendance for some is precluded by health issues or advancing age. But most believers are able to be in church with some degree of regularity, yet a disturbing number simply choose not to come. Why? I'm sure there are many reasons, but one simple one is that it's easier and less demanding to be home alone.

With this backdrop in mind, let's briefly look at five essential reasons why you need to stay connected, especially in treacherous, uncertain times like these.

"AS WE SEE THE DAY APPROACHING"

The first reason we need to stay connected is in Hebrews 10:24-25. This passage addresses the need to live in meaningful community with one another as we wait for the Lord's coming in these last days. It's a clarion call to connect in light of Christ's coming. It's a last-days strategy for spiritual survival:

Let us think of ways to motivate one another to acts
of love and good works. And let us not neglect our
meeting together, as some people do, but encourage

one another, especially now that the day of his return
is drawing near.

Anyone who reads the newspaper, watches cable news,
or follows world events online realizes our world is on fire.
The Middle East remains a global hot spot. Israel is in the
crosshairs. North Korea is a nuclear menace. The Russian
Bear is roaring out of hibernation. Even those with a super-
ficial knowledge of end-times prophecy realize this world
seems to be getting near closing time. Many signs seem
to be aligning, giving us every reason to believe the coming of Christ is near. No one on earth knows the time of
Christ's coming, but as believers, we're to live looking, with
an attitude of expectancy concerning our Lord's coming (see
1 Thessalonians 1:10).

This hope and anticipation should energize every believer
with a renewed sense of urgency to be about the Lord's business. Hebrews 10:25 clearly states that a key aspect of that
business is to stay connected with one another through the
fellowship of the local church. The words "the day of his
return is drawing near" or "as you see the Day approaching"
(as in NIV) indicate that believers today should be gathering
together *more* frequently, not less, as we see the approach of
the Lord's coming. With all that's happening in our world
today, churches should be packed. As signs of the times proliferate, church attendance should be soaring. Yet, sadly, we
see the exact opposite. Malaise and indifference have set in.

Do you remember what it was like in the wake of the

terrorist attack on 9/11? Churches were filled to capacity and in many cases overfilled. Faced with the fragility of life, people sought solace in God and reevaluated what's important. However, the spike in attendance waned as life got back to normal. People settled into a pattern that fails to prioritize regular attendance at public worship.

There's a humorous, well-worn, but worthwhile illustration about a church that announced "a special 'No Excuse Sunday'" to "make it possible for everyone to attend church" on a specific Lord's Day. The announcement contained the following incentives:

> Cots will be placed in the foyer for those who say, "Sunday is my only day to sleep."
> We will have steel helmets for those who say, "The roof will cave in if I ever come to church."
> Blankets will be furnished for those who think the church is too cold and fans for those who think the church is too hot.
> We will have hearing aids for those who think the preacher speaks too softly and cotton for those who think he preaches too loudly.
> Scorecards will be available for those who wish to list the hypocrites present.
> Some relatives will be in attendance for those who like to go visiting on Sunday.
> There will be TV dinners for those who can't go to church and cook dinner also.

> One section will be devoted to trees and grass for those who like to see God in nature.
> Finally, the sanctuary will be decorated with both Christmas poinsettias and Easter lilies for those who have never seen the church without them.[10]

Ouch! That hits pretty close to home for a growing number of contemporary churchgoers. The writer of Hebrews leaves no doubt that regular attendance of public worship is not an option for believers; it's a command. When it comes to the church, assembly is required. Regardless of this stern admonition, more and more professing Christians fail to take church attendance seriously. Hebrews 10:25 calls on us to gather for mutual encouragement as we see the day drawing near. In troubled times, we all need encouragement. We need encouragement to read our Bibles, to pray, to love our spouses, to sacrifice for others, to share, to tell others about Jesus, and to turn from sin. For me, as a pastor, just seeing God's people on Sunday morning is an encouragement. Your simple presence is a much greater encouragement to others, especially your pastor, than you will ever know.

The call to assemble is urgent. As Erwin Lutzer says, "Never before in American history has it been so important to become an active part of a network of other believers for worship, encouragement, instruction, and prayer. Bible studies, prayer groups, and discipleship training of believers to be change-agents in their world."[11]

The church is a place of safety and protection as believers

come under the supervision and care of pastors who look out for their well-being (see Hebrews 13:17). Failing to have a church home and meet with God's people regularly leaves you isolated, alone, and exposed, and strays from the herd are always the easiest for the lions to pick off. Far too many believers today are voluntarily leaving themselves and their families spiritually exposed outside the church in the devil's domain. I like the story author Anne Lamott tells about a seven-year-old girl who got lost in a big city:

> The girl frantically ran up and down several streets, looking for a familiar landmark. A policeman saw the girl, realized something was wrong, and offered to help. So she got in the car and he slowly drove through nearby neighborhoods. Suddenly the girl pointed to a church and asked the policeman to let her out. She assured him, "This is my church, and I can always find my way home from here."[12]

As the world darkens and Christ's coming draws near, never have so many needed to find their way home, especially in the millennial generation. Encouraging them to regularly be a part of corporate worship and fellowship is a strong beginning point.

WHEN THE CHURCH WAS YOUNG

The second, and perhaps the simplest, reason we need to stay connected with other believers is the pattern in the early church. The emphasis on connection is present in the very first church in Jerusalem a few weeks after the resurrection of Christ:

> They were continually devoting themselves to the apostles' teaching and to fellowship, to the breaking of bread and to prayer.
> Everyone kept feeling a sense of awe; and many wonders and signs were taking place through the apostles. And all those who had believed were together and had all things in common; and they began selling their property and possessions and were sharing them with all, as anyone might have need. Day by day continuing with one mind in the temple, and breaking bread from house to house, they were taking their meals together with gladness and sincerity of heart, praising God and having favor with all the people. And the Lord was adding to their number day by day those who were being saved.
>
> ACTS 2:42-47, NASB

The first point mentioned in this snapshot of the early church is the apostles' teaching, which is foundational to everything else. We must gather to hear God's Word or our fellowship is little more than a social gathering. The truth is what ties us together. The faithful preaching of God's Word is the heart muscle of the church, which pumps life into everything else we do. We rally around a common gospel, centered in our great Savior. But these verses in Acts 2 also focus repeatedly on the gathering together of God's people. We're not just *believers*; we're *belongers*.

Notice also that there's a beautiful balance here between the corporate gatherings of the church in the Temple area and smaller, private gatherings for meals in individual homes. We observe this throughout the book of Acts, which establishes a pattern for our gatherings today.

You and I need the corporate church setting to sing and praise God together, to pray, to learn, and to celebrate the Lord's Supper and baptism. There's something about the power of presence. Just being with God's people every week is a strong encouragement. Seeing young families with young children worshiping the Lord; watching people singing, giving, and praying together; and observing the church surrounding those who are dealing with physical ailments or old age are all part of growing deeper in our shared life in Christ.

We also need to connect with other believers in smaller gatherings for meaningful fellowship and discipleship. Hebrews 10:24-25 says we must gather regularly to "spur one another on toward love and good deeds" (NIV). While this can and should happen as we sing and listen to the preaching of God's Word in a corporate setting, in the deepest sense this happens in smaller gatherings.

These smaller gatherings take many forms such as home groups, lunch meetings, women's or men's Bible studies, adult Sunday school classes, and so on. I've even heard about one church that had a group of older men who called themselves ROMEOs (Retired Old Men Eating Out) who met regularly for Christian fellowship.

At the church I pastor, we have ABFs (Adult Bible Fellowship groups) that meet on Sunday mornings at parallel times with our corporate worship services. While it may appear in many forms, small-group ministry is an integral ingredient for healthy spiritual growth.

Of course, in all of this, our goal is not just to get people to church more and keep them busy meeting in more intimate settings. Church attendance and connection is a means, not an end. The end is a growing, thriving, maturing walk with Jesus Christ.

The story is told that a pastor who was new to a small Oklahoma town started his tenure as pastor by stopping by the houses of the church's members and inviting them to come to church the following Sunday. When Sunday rolled around, however, he was disappointed to discover that the members he had invited weren't there and the church was mostly empty. The next week he took out an ad in the local newspaper, inviting people to the funeral of the church.

When the time for the funeral came, the church was packed because people were curious how a funeral for a building might work. A hearse arrived, and pallbearers carried the casket into the sanctuary and placed it in front of the pulpit.

The pastor gave a eulogy for the church, and afterward he opened the casket's lid for the congregation to pay their respects. The people didn't know what to expect—what could possibly be in the casket to represent a dead church?—so they dutifully approached the casket. And once each person looked in, they saw it: their own reflection. The "dead church" was a mirror.

The death of a church is the death of the people because a church is not a building or an organization—a church is its people. And each church is a reflection of the spiritual vitality of those who claim membership there.

How is your church doing? In many ways your church is a mirror image of you. What does the mirror say about you and your family?

Let me add one point here. All pastors, elders, and church leaders must do all we can in our local churches to provide a setting that encourages God's people to join us. God has commanded all Christians not to forsake assembling together, but we must do all we can to remove as many obstacles as possible and to make it edifying for people to come. God's Word must be preached accurately, clearly, and practically. Our singing must glorify God and flow from passionate hearts. Our fellowship must be enriched by the Lord's presence. The sheep are called to gather, but the shepherds must work hard to make sure the sheep find green pastures that nourish their souls. I love the saying "The world at its worst needs the church at its best." Few would dispute that our world today is at its worst. What we're witnessing is nothing short of tragic. This should provide ample motivation for us to be at our best when we're gathered together on the Lord's

Day and then take that with us as we're unleashed into the community throughout the week.

TAKING SIDES

The third reason for us to take our connection to the church seriously as the end draws near is that as church attendance becomes increasingly spotty and intermittent in our culture, one of the ways we give witness to our love for Christ is by going to church. Those who connect frequently with God's people give visible evidence of their commitment to Christ and his Word to their neighbors and friends. Of course, we all know that going to church can be perfunctory and routine and has no saving merit, but what I'm talking about is not duty but delight. Being a real part of a local church with a sense of expectancy and excitement each week testifies to a watching world that we belong to Jesus and love him.

In some ways, attending church is a litmus test of our loyalty to Christ. It's a birthmark and benchmark for believers. Think about it. If we aren't loyal to Christ in something as simple as showing up for church on the Lord's Day, how committed are we in other, more demanding aspects of our faith such as giving sacrificially, serving, praying, reading God's Word, or sharing the gospel with others? Going to church consistently should be the bare minimum—the lowest rung—of our Christian commitment. If we can't carve out time from our schedules to regularly meet for public worship, how likely are we to make deeper sacrifices for our Lord?

Doug McIntosh, in his book *Life's Greatest Journey*, tells

the story of an elderly man who lost his hearing late in life. Despite his hearing loss and inability to hear the songs being sung or words being spoken, he attended church every week. When one of his neighbors asked why he continued to go to church when he couldn't hear what was happening, he simply replied, "I want people to know whose side I'm on."[13]

Going to church can never wash away our sins or, by itself, make us more righteous, but increasingly in our culture it does show our friends and neighbors "whose side we're on."

PICTURING THE CHURCH

Fourth, the New Testament employs many metaphors to describe the church of Jesus Christ that stress our closeness to Jesus and to one another and how much we need each other.

Here are a few of the most basic ones:

> Body (see 1 Corinthians 12): Jesus is the Head; we are the various parts.
> Flock (see John 10:11-15): Jesus is the Shepherd; we are the sheep.
> Building (see Ephesians 2:20-21; 1 Peter 2:5): Jesus is the Cornerstone; we are the stones cemented together.
> Vine (see John 15:1-11): Jesus is the Vine; we are the branches.

Each of these metaphors involves close connection to Jesus and others. We were never intended to live and grow in isolation from other believers. These images also reveal that together we are much more than we could ever be alone. The church is much greater than the sum of its parts.

Nevertheless, going it alone is becoming more common. More and more people claim they're finding all they need online. They stay home and watch a sermon on Sunday and check the worship box for the week. But listening to a sermon online is not enough. Certainly, times have changed since the first century, and we have wonderful, helpful technology that was not available then. Watching sermons online is a great way to keep up with what's going on at your church when you're ill or out of town. That said, sitting at home in front of your computer every Saturday evening or Sunday morning is not what the New Testament envisions for church connection. Spiritual growth and encouragement take place in the context of actual, lived community.

As David Jeremiah says, "Cyber-community seems nice until something bad happens, and then we want face time rather than Facebook."[14] Certainly, in today's world, social media is a great way to stay in touch with others, but the church is a face-to-face community that can never be replaced by Facebook. The pulpit can seem far away during the week. There's no substitute for real community with other believers.

I like the old story about the pastor who visited a member of his church who had stopped attending without giving a reason. The pastor visited the man on a cold evening when the man was home alone, warming himself in front of the fireplace. The man invited the pastor to sit with him and waited for the pastor to lecture him about his church attendance. However, instead of talking, the pastor took the tongs by the fireplace and picked up a burning ember and placed it off to the side, all by itself. The pastor remained silent in all of this, which made the man uncomfortable, so he fixed his attention on the ember whose flame was quietly dimming and then extinguished.

After the ember had been dead for a few minutes, the pastor placed it back in the fire, where it immediately ignited. When the pastor made a move to leave, his host said, "Thank you so much for your visit and especially for the fiery sermon. I'll be back in church next Sunday."[15]

The truth is we cool spiritually and eventually stop glowing without the warmth of our brothers and sisters in Christ. We need each other more than we often realize.

Make sure you stay on fire and spread the heat to others, and do it even more as we see the day approaching. You need the church, and the church needs you. Don't get isolated and exposed.

Your spiritual survival, and that of your family, is at stake in these last days when the world is at its worst.

"ONE ANOTHERING"

A fifth reason to stay connected is found in the many New Testament commands about how we live in connection with one another. The commands in these verses are often referred to as "one anothering."

The New Testament records many "one anothers." Some

are repeated several times, so there are about thirty-three unique "one anothers." Here are a few of the main ones. (Note that the New Living Translation usually translates this phrase as "each other.")

> "Love each other" (John 15:12)
> "Wash each other's feet" (John 13:14)
> "Love each other with genuine affection, and take delight in honoring each other" (Romans 12:10)
> "Live in harmony with each other" (Romans 12:16)
> "Build each other up" (Romans 14:19)
> "Accept each other just as Christ has accepted you" (Romans 15:7)
> "Teach each other" (Romans 15:14)
> "Greet each other with a sacred kiss" (Romans 16:16)
> "Wait [to eat the Lord's Supper] for each other" (1 Corinthians 11:33)
> "Care for each other" (1 Corinthians 12:25)
> "Serve one another" (Galatians 5:13)
> "Share each other's burdens" (Galatians 6:2)
> "Be patient with each other" (Ephesians 4:2)
> "We are members of one another" (Ephesians 4:25, NASB)
> "Be kind to each other, tenderhearted, forgiving one another" (Ephesians 4:32)
> "Submit to one another" (Ephesians 5:21)
> "Regard one another as more important than yourselves" (Philippians 2:3, NASB)

> "Encourage each other with these words [about Jesus' return]" (1 Thessalonians 4:18)
> "Encourage each other and build each other up" (1 Thessalonians 5:11)
> "Think of ways to motivate one another to acts of love and good works," "not neglect our meeting together, . . . but encourage one another" (Hebrews 10:24-25)
> "Confess your sins to each other and pray for each other" (James 5:16)
> "Be hospitable to one another" (1 Peter 4:9, NASB)[16]

We sometimes forget that "one anothering" can only be faithfully fulfilled if we are regularly *with* one another. First Thessalonians 5:11 summarizes this idea beautifully. It literally says, "Build up one the one," that is, "one by one." We build up God's people one by one. This is true even in large settings in the church. Ultimately, all ministry is personal and individual. People are built up one by one. We need each other and the community of mutual support to survive and grow spiritually. God and his transformative grace are most evident in the sphere of a loving community. We need each other. Our salvation is personal, but it is not private.

There's an old poem sometimes attributed to William Blake that says this well:

I sought my soul, and my soul eluded me.
I sought my God, and my God I could not see.
I sought my brother, and I found all three.

DEADLY DISCONNECT

Sunandha Kumariratana was the queen of Thailand in the late nineteenth century. Among the laws in that day was one forbidding anyone to touch the queen under threat of death.

While she was journeying to the summer palace with her young daughter on May 31, 1880, the royal boat they were traveling in capsized. There were many witnesses to the capsizing, but they were unwilling to pull her from the watery grave because of the law. A guard on another boat even reiterated the law that the queen was not to be touched. As a result, the queen drowned.[17]

Isolating yourself from others is dangerous and can even be deadly. If you keep others away and never let them touch your life, when you're drowning, they may not be able to come to your aid.

Don't drown needlessly in discouragement, sorrow, grief, loneliness, pain, and trouble. Meet with God's people regularly, joyfully, and often. Allow others to connect with you, and be willing and eager to reach out and touch the lives of others in meaningful ways.

And do it all the more as "the day of his return is drawing near."

Your spiritual health and survival hangs in the balance.

CHAPTER 4

PUT ON YOUR ARMOR

*Two things are happening today that I never thought I would
live to see. First, spiritual warfare is getting much more intense as
Satan's attacks become bolder. Second . . . too many Christians
are not taking spiritual warfare seriously or even
believing such a war is going on.*

DAVID JEREMIAH

GUN SALES IN AMERICA TODAY are on the rise. The worse the
news gets, the more people seem to buy—many in preparation for what may lie ahead. Television shows like *Doomsday
Preppers* and *The Wheel* fuel the fear of some apocalyptic scenario that showcases the need to be armed and ready.

I was talking to a friend of mine a while back when some
especially bad news was in the headlines. We were talking
about people buying gold to shield themselves from potential
market crashes or collapses. He told me, "I'm not buying
gold; I'm buying lead." That seems to be a shared sentiment.
Increasingly, many are stocking up on food, guns, ammo, and
anything else they think can help them survive the uncertain
days ahead.

More and more people today are responding to world
events out of panic, fear, and an unhealthy obsession about

some impending catastrophe. They're focused on being armed and dangerous. But the most important way to arm and protect yourself and your family in these uncertain times is to be armed spiritually. Increasing numbers of people have a small arsenal of physical weaponry but don't have enough spiritual power or protection to match an airsoft gun.

With surging spiritual deception and demonic forces arrayed against us as Christ's coming draws near, every believer needs to be spiritually armed to the teeth. If we fail in this, we are easy prey for the enemy of our souls. The Bible is clear. As the Lord's coming draws near, as the last days run their course, every believer in Jesus Christ needs to be equipped with the full armor of God:

> This is all the more urgent, for you know how late it is; time is running out. Wake up, for our salvation is nearer now than when we first believed. The night is almost gone; the day of salvation will soon be here. So remove your dark deeds like dirty clothes, and put on the shining armor of right living. Because we belong to the day, we must live decent lives for all to see. Don't participate in the darkness of wild parties and drunkenness, or in sexual promiscuity and immoral living, or in quarreling and jealousy. Instead, clothe yourself with the presence of the Lord Jesus Christ. And don't let yourself think about ways to indulge your evil desires.
>
> ROMANS 13:11-14

These verses are clear that, as the last days draw to a close, we must put on the spiritual armor of light. Without it, we're defenseless. Many passages in the New Testament call believers to "take up arms" spiritually in these last days, but Ephesians 6:10-18 is the central passage on our spiritual warfare as believers. Please read these words slowly and thoughtfully:

> Be strong in the Lord and in his mighty power. Put on the full armor of God, so that you can take your stand against the devil's schemes. For our struggle is not against flesh and blood, but against the rulers, against the authorities, against the powers of this dark world and against the spiritual forces of evil in the heavenly realms. Therefore put on the full armor of God, so that when the day of evil comes, you may be able to stand your ground, and after you have done everything, to stand. Stand firm then, with the belt of truth buckled around your waist, with the breastplate of righteousness in place, and with your feet fitted with the readiness that comes from the gospel of peace. In addition to all this, take up the shield of faith, with which you can extinguish all the flaming arrows of the evil one. Take the helmet of salvation and the sword of the Spirit, which is the word of God.
>
> And pray in the Spirit on all occasions with all kinds of prayers and requests. With this in mind, be alert and always keep on praying for all the Lord's people. (NIV)

THE INVISIBLE WAR

Every believer in Christ senses that he or she faces daily conflict. We all recognize this relentless reality. We have our sin nature on the inside that exerts a strong gravitational pull toward sin and the wicked world around us that draws us to compromise with its values and attitudes.

Nevertheless, many are not aware of the invisible war in the spirit realm that rages around us, or worse yet, they may choose to ignore it. Our secular world today is increasingly a "world without windows."[1] Secularists believe the unseen is unreal. Yet we deny the unseen world at our own peril. As Lesslie Newbigin warns, "The principalities and powers are realities. We may not be able to visualize them, to locate them, or to say exactly what they are. But we are foolish if we pretend they do not exist."[2]

Just beyond the thin veil of this visible world is a spiritual world every bit as real. Beyond the paper-thin walls of this fading world is a cosmic struggle encircling us. Understanding this invisible war helps us see things as they really are.

You could hardly find a better statement of the Christian life and our spiritual combat than this: "The ideal war is one that no one realizes war is being waged, that is mostly invisible, not because its actions are camouflaged, but because they look like something else. War need never be declared again because we are always at war."[3] It's like modern terrorism. We're always at war, but it's mostly invisible.

Satan is the ultimate terrorist who led the first rebellion, the first insurgency in history as he was lifted up in pride.

When he fell into sin, he went on a campaign in heaven to slander God and recruited one-third of the angelic host to join his conspiracy (see Ezekiel 28:15-17; Revelation 12:4). These fallen angels are what the Scriptures refer to as demons. There is only one devil, but there are many demons. They are our enemies in the invisible war.

The intensity of the cosmic conflict is underscored by the word "struggle" in Ephesians 6:12, which in ancient times referred to wrestling in the Greek games. The picture of wrestling emphasizes the closeness of the conflict and the sustained effort and stamina required in this fight. Moreover, the word "against" occurs six times in Ephesians 6:10-12, which underlines the opposition we face in this cosmic clash of forces and the intensity of the struggle. The Lord wants us to know that we're up against a real enemy. The battle lines are clearly drawn. God and his people are on one side; Satan and his demons are on the other. Ray Stedman vividly describes this war:

> Spiritual warfare is not about the struggle of man against man. It is not a political struggle, a social struggle, an economic struggle, or even a religious-theological-doctrinal struggle. It is not a struggle *between* human beings. It is a struggle *within* human beings. . . . The battle is not against people, but against unseen spiritual powers. In fact, the entire human race is under a vicious assault by certain principalities and powers, world rulers of darkness,

wicked spirits in high places. . . . Every man, every woman, every child, everywhere is a target of the enemy. The devil has each one of us in his crosshairs. The whole race is opposed by the principalities and powers, the world rulers of this present darkness.[4]

The good news in this war is that, according to the Bible, Satan and his minions are a defeated foe. The Lord Jesus, our Commander in Chief, crushed Satan's head at the Cross. Nevertheless, though Satan is infinitely mismatched and has no chance of winning, he furiously fights the Lord and his people, working to undermine our faith and hinder our progress in the Christian life. Satan's doom is sure. His eternal incarceration in the lake of fire is recorded in Revelation 20:10. However, that defeat is yet to be fully consummated at the second coming of Christ. In the meantime we fight our enemy not *for* victory but *from* victory.

Jesus has won the victory for us already. He has taken the spiritual high ground staked out in Ephesians 1–3. All that's left for us is to hold the spiritual ground he has gained on our behalf. The purpose of our spiritual armor is not to attack Satan or gain new territory. Notice that the key word "stand" punctuates Ephesians 6:10-13 four times. The same idea of "standing" (holding our ground) and "resisting" is found elsewhere in the New Testament in reference to our warfare against Satan and his host. James 4:7 says, "Resist the devil, and he will flee from you." First Peter 5:9, referring to Satan, concurs: "Resist him, firm in your faith" (NASB).

SUIT UP

To protect us in our battle with the enemy, God has graciously provided us with a spiritual suit of armor because we are defenseless in ourselves and our own strength. We are no match for the forces of evil. As S. Lewis Johnson says, "You notice the Apostle does not say, 'be strong in human plans.' He does not say, 'be strong in human methods.' He does not say, 'be strong in the latest ideas' that sweep over the evangelical church, but 'be strong in the Lord and the power of his might.'"[5] What every believer needs is the Lord. We don't need him and our own strength and ingenuity; we need him and his provision.

Before we identify and describe each individual piece of our "armor," I want to make a few general observations about our equipment. First, we must avail ourselves of the armor God has provided. The spiritual battle we're facing is an epic struggle pitted against Satan and his angels, against the principalities and powers—it is being fought every day right where we live, in our homes, our offices, our marriages, our churches, and in the inner core of our hearts. The Bible is clear that God has provided us with resources to win this war, but we must take advantage of his provision. We have to "take [it] up" and "put [it] on." The armor doesn't cover us automatically. We have to put it on daily.

Second, we must put on *all* the armor. We can't decide which pieces to put on and which to leave off. Every piece is essential. It's the *full* armor—the complete "panoply." The Welsh preacher Martyn Lloyd-Jones notes,

If you are to be a soldier in this army, if you are to fight victoriously in this crusade, you have to put on the entire equipment given to you. That is a rule in any army. . . . And that is infinitely more true in this spiritual realm and warfare with which we are concerned. . . . You need it all . . . because your understanding is inadequate. It is God alone who knows your enemy, and He knows exactly the provision that is essential to you if you are to continue standing. Every single part and portion of this armour is absolutely essential; and the first thing you have to learn is that you are not in a position to pick and choose.[6]

We need all the armor if we're going to stand firm in these last days.

Third, we need to wear *all* the armor *all* the time. We never know when the enemy will strike, so the only way to be prepared is to always have it on. Around 1171, John de Courcy conquered land in Northern Ireland. John was a courageous warrior who was serious about the worship of God and gave God the glory for his victories. King John in England wanted to capture and kill him but knew it would be very difficult because de Courcy was such a fierce warrior. King John commissioned Sir Hugh de Lacy to find out how to capture de Courcy. To learn about de Courcy's habits and weaknesses, Hugh de Lacy conferred with certain of de Courcy's own men as to how he might be taken, and they said it was not possible since he always wore his armor. The only time each year when he took off his armor in public was Good Friday. His custom on that day was to wear no armor and carry no shield or weapon. He walked around the church five times barefoot and then spent the rest of the day in church, kneeling in prayer. Hugh de Lacy determined that Good Friday was the only opening to capture de Courcy, and so on that day a group of his men descended suddenly upon him. De Courcy found nothing but a cross pole to defend himself and slew thirteen men until it broke. Finally, with no armor and no weapon, the great warrior was captured. In the brief time when he was defenseless, the enemy struck.

Our enemy is no different. His sinister surveillance of our lives is cunning and constant, so we can be sure he knows when we're not wearing our armor. He picks his time when we least expect it and stand unprepared. We have to put the armor on, and we have to put it all on all the time. Without it, we're easy prey.

With these thoughts in mind, let's turn our attention to the individual pieces of our spiritual defense system.

THE BELT OF TRUTH

The pieces of our spiritual armor listed in the New Testament are adapted from the equipment worn in that day by a Roman hoplite, or foot soldier. Paul takes something his audience would have been familiar with and invests it with spiritual meaning. The parallels are striking.

The first piece of the Roman soldier's armor was his belt,

which was the first thing he would put on to prepare for battle. No soldier could fight effectively without his belt. It was six inches wide and made of either leather or linen. The belt served two important functions. First, the Roman hoplite would use the belt to gird his loins, which refers to tucking his tunic under his belt so he could move freely and fight effectively without getting his legs and feet tangled in it. Getting tripped up in battle was deadly. Second, the belt supported his weapons. The sword hung from it. Archers used it to attach their quivers of arrows.

With this background, it makes sense that our spiritual armor begins with truth because God's truth is what enables us to move freely and holds everything else together. Truth must come first. Satan is a deceiver—the father of lies. Satan's master campaign of deception is to attack the Word of God. He will do anything he can to undermine it and deceive people. Everything in our lives hangs on our knowledge and application of God's truth.

But how do we put on the belt of truth? Here are a couple of practical thoughts:

> *Listen to good Bible exposition.* Regularly attend a church that teaches biblical truth faithfully and systematically, meditate on what you hear, and apply it to your life. If there's no Bible-teaching church in your town, attend the best church you can find. You can supplement what's lacking by listening to faithful preachers on local Christian radio or downloaded sermons.

> *Read and study the Bible on your own.* Get into a good Bible study where you can encourage others in the truth and be encouraged. One important point to note in Ephesians 6 is that all the verbs and pronouns in this section are in the plural, which of course means that this all applies to every believer. But it also indicates to us that we aren't alone. We're in God's army together. We're a band of brothers and sisters. We are struggling side by side, arm in arm, shoulder to shoulder. We stand for God's truth together. Seeing others standing firm and resisting the devil shores up our own faith and gives us the resolve to hold our ground.

Doing these things will cinch your belt tighter and tighter each day.

THE BREASTPLATE OF RIGHTEOUSNESS

No Roman soldier would ever think of going into battle without his breastplate. This essential armor was a tough, sleeveless garment of leather or heavy linen that protected his full torso, and sewed on it were overlapping slices of animal hooves or horns or pieces of metal for extra reinforcement. Sometimes a breastplate was made of molded metal that conformed to the body. It was like a modern bulletproof vest or body armor. The purpose was obviously to cover lungs and other vital organs, the heart most of all.

Likewise, our hearts are protected against the accusations and condemnation of the enemy by righteousness. The righteousness here is not our own but that of Jesus Christ, which has been credited to us (see 2 Corinthians 5:21). Knowing about this righteousness and appropriating it by faith protects us against the onslaught of the enemy. One of Satan's favorite attacks on our hearts is false accusations. He's "the accuser of our brethren" (Revelation 12:10, NASB). The word "devil" (*diabolos*) means "accuser" or "slanderer." Our protection against the bombardment of accusation and condemnation is the righteousness of Jesus Christ. We rest in his merits—in his righteousness alone (see Romans 8:1, 33). Knowing that we stand accepted before God, not condemned, gives us great fortitude to stand our ground.

THE SHOES OF PEACE

The image of shoes comes from the Roman soldier's *caliga*, or war boot, which was the half-boot worn by Roman legionnaires. It was an open-toed leather boot, tightly fastened to the ankles and shins with leather straps and stuffed with wool or fur in cold weather. These shoes weren't for running (pursuing or fleeing from the enemy); rather, these thick-soled boots were made for long marches and a solid stance. The key in battle was keeping your footing during close combat. The bottoms of the boots were covered with sharp spikes or nails to give traction, enabling the warrior to make quick, sudden moves without slipping and falling.

In warfare, shoes are critical. They're the foundation. They provide stability. Imagine a Roman soldier in armor from head to foot but with no shoes. The ground would quickly tear his feet to shreds, and he would easily lose traction, rendering him helpless.

So, what provides the firm foundation we need for spiritual warfare? What gives us the readiness we need—the preparation that will make us immovable in the battle? Ephesians 6:15 talks about "feet fitted with the readiness that comes from the gospel of peace" (NIV). The peace we have with God through the gospel makes us immovable. Paul refers to this peace earlier in Ephesians 2, and even writes, "Christ himself has brought peace to us" (verse 14).

Scripture tells us that before we were converted, we were enemies of God. We were at war with him, but the death of Christ brought peace (see Romans 5:1, 10). When we trust Christ as our Savior, we are justified by faith. The result is that we have peace with God. This is the gospel of peace. Peace with God is our new position in Christ. And it's on the basis of this new position that we are able to resist the forces of Satan. This is our foundation and footing. When our feet are planted in this peace, we can stand firm against the malicious assaults of the enemy.

THE SHIELD OF FAITH

Ephesians 6:16 says, "In addition to all this, take up the shield of faith, with which you can extinguish all the flaming arrows of the evil one" (NIV). The other pieces of armor up to this point are fastened to the body, but here the shield must be picked up. The word for "shield" used here doesn't refer to the small, round shield we see in movies like *Gladiator* but to a large, oblong one that was four feet tall, two and one-half feet wide, and as thick as a person's hand. When Satan and his forces fire their flaming missiles of doubt, they are extinguished by our faith. Again, 1 Peter 5:9 says, "Resist him, firm in your faith" (NASB).

One other interesting feature of the Roman shield is that it had hooks on each side to join to the shields of others. In the same way, we join our faith with other believers in times of attack to form an impenetrable wall of protection. If we're honest, we all have to admit that sometimes in the fog of spiritual warfare it's easy to feel alone and isolated and give way to discouragement or even depression. The enemy works to magnify this in our lives. Let's never forget to lock shields with our brothers and sisters in Christ—joining our faith with theirs. We must never forget that we're not in the battle alone. We need to stay in close ranks with other believers as the end draws near (see Hebrews 10:25).

THE HELMET OF SALVATION

Every Roman soldier wore a helmet made of bronze or iron, lined inside with felt or sponge to make it tolerable to wear for long periods of time. Nothing is more vital in battle than protecting the brain from battering blows. Applying this to our spiritual lives, guarding our minds is essential in the invisible war. Nothing is more important than keeping our thinking straight and clear. Let's face it—we live in cloudy, chaotic times. The Niagara of negative news—from political polarization to the growing threat of nuclear war—can easily drive us to discouragement and even despair. A sense of gloom seems to hang in the air. Satan and his forces seize this to swamp us with hopelessness.

But the believer in Christ has the helmet of salvation. We have a resource that protects our mind—that keeps us thinking straight in confusing times. That piece of equipment is salvation, more specifically, our future salvation that will be realized when Jesus comes. As Ray Stedman writes,

> [The apostle Paul] is not talking about the salvation of the soul. He is not referring to salvation as regeneration or conversion. In other words, he is not looking backwards, to the moment of conversion. The first three pieces of armor do so, but the next three pieces of armor, including the helmet of salvation, look forward, not back. Paul is talking about a salvation that will be a future event.[7]

The helmet of salvation is final, full salvation or deliverance when the Lord Jesus returns to earth. This understanding is confirmed by 1 Thessalonians 5:8, which refers to the believer's helmet as the "confidence of our salvation" (see also Romans 13:11). Stedman continues,

> [Paul] is talking about the day of the return of Christ, the day when creation will be delivered from bondage by Christ's return to establish His kingdom. This helmet, therefore, is the recognition that . . . the plan of God is moving forward, right on schedule. Jesus

Christ is coming back, and He will appear again, and He will establish His own reign in righteousness on the earth. That is the helmet of salvation which will keep your thinking straight in the hour of man's utter confusion and darkness. . . . If you can keep God's eternal plan in view at all times, it will save you from enormous heartache and fear as you read your daily newspaper. When you see the chaos in the world, you will know that even the disorder that Satan seeks to stir up in the world is being used to further God's plan and bring His kingdom one day nearer. Though we are often shocked whenever we open a newspaper or turn on CNN, God is never surprised. His plan is right on schedule.[8]

God has a plan, and it is on schedule. Every day that passes, its completion is one day nearer. Our hope is not in man but in God. Our knowledge of our future salvation keeps our thinking straight and stable. Keeping God's eternal plan in view will keep you from a great deal of heartache and fear.

That's one of the reasons I believe it's so important to regularly preach and teach on the Lord's coming. We need to be reminded often that Jesus is coming again to bring our salvation to its consummation.

THE SWORD OF THE SPIRIT

The first five items in our spiritual arsenal are defensive in nature. The only offensive weapon listed in Ephesians 6 is the Bible, the Word of God. Picture a Roman warrior with all his armor firmly in place, shoes laced up, and carrying his massive shield on his left arm, yet with no weapon in his right hand. A massacre would ensue. A warrior with no weapon is easily dispatched.

Similarly, every Christian warrior must have a weapon for the war against the spiritual forces of darkness, and that powerful weapon is "the sword of the Spirit, which is the word of God" (see also Hebrews 4:12-13). The Greek word for "sword" refers to the Roman short sword, which was essentially a large knife with a two-edged blade, two inches wide and about sixteen to eighteen inches long. As you can imagine, this was used in hand-to-hand combat. This reinforces the reality of the up-close nature of the spiritual conflict.

Our sword is God's Word. The Word of God cuts, convicts, challenges, and confronts. It's razor sharp. As someone has said, "It's all edge." This helps explain why the Word of God is under sustained attack by the enemy. Satan has relentlessly attacked the Bible down through the ages because it's the one weapon that cuts through his deception and neutralizes his temptations. Satan is at war with the Word of God because he knows its power.

The power of the Word rises from its source. It's called the "sword of the *Spirit*." The Spirit is the Voice who inspired God's Word (see 2 Timothy 3:16). Human authors wrote the words of Scripture through their own unique personality, vocabulary, and background, but behind the entire process the Spirit worked in such a way that the words inscribed on

THE END TIMES SURVIVAL GUIDE

the page were the very words of God himself (see 2 Peter 1:21). That's why the Bible is so powerful and precious. Every word is inspired or breathed out by the Holy Spirit.

One more point concerning our sword is important. The term used for God's Word (*rhema*) refers to a particular, specific saying of Scripture. For instance, John 3:16 is a *rhema*; Romans 3:23 is a *rhema*. A *rhema* is God's Word applied to a specific situation in your life. Thinking of it this way means the Bible is like an armory in itself, and inside are all kinds of swords you can pull out when you need to go on the offensive against the enemy. When you select the right sword, it slices through everything, right to the heart of the matter.

As James Boice says, "According to Ephesians 6:17, you must know the specific sayings of Scripture—you must have them memorized—if you are to resist and overcome Satan successfully. . . . Satan will not flee from us simply because we tell him to. . . . There is nothing in all life more powerful than the specific words of God."[9]

Jesus perfectly modeled this for us when he was tempted by the devil in the wilderness for forty days (see Matthew 4:1-11). During this duel in the desert, Jesus deftly wielded the Word of God. Each time Satan launched his assault, Jesus responded with "It is written" and quoted a specific verse from the Old Testament book of Deuteronomy. He slashed the temptations to pieces with his sword, totally disarming Satan. Out of ammunition, the defeated devil left Jesus. There's one vital point here we dare not miss—if Jesus used Scripture as his weapon, how much more should we?

78

Where is your sword all week? Is it safely in the sheath, sitting on the shelf? Or is it in your hand, ready to attack when needed?

Part of the legend of King Arthur is his famous sword known as Excalibur. When the Lady of the Lake brings the sword up from the water, presenting it to Arthur, there's an engraving on opposite sides of the blade—"take me up" and "cast me away." We face these same two options every day with our own Excalibur—the Bible. Our spiritual survival hangs in the balance depending upon which choice we make. Will we take it up and read it, or will we cast it away?

WARFARE PRAYER

I'm no expert on military tactics or strategy, but even I know that in modern warfare, victory or defeat turns on one key factor: who controls the skies. It's all about air power. Whoever wins the air wins the war.

The same is true in the invisible war. Air superiority is decisive. Fittingly, our spiritual armor concludes with a call to control the air with our prayers. Ephesians 6:18 says, "Pray in the Spirit at all times and on every occasion. Stay alert and be persistent in your prayers for all believers everywhere."

Prayer is our secret weapon in the invisible war, and it's something every Christian can do. Prayer requires no special training, no great knowledge, and no special degree of spiritual maturity. All of us can humbly approach the Lord and ask for what we need.

Whatever else you do, pray. There is no victory over the enemy without it.

PUT ON JESUS

We've said quite a bit about our spiritual survival suit in this chapter, but to make it as simple as possible, essentially, the armor is Jesus Christ. Romans 13:12 tells us to "put on the armor of light" (NASB), and then Romans 13:14 says "put on the Lord Jesus Christ" (NASB). In other words, we are to dress up in Jesus.

As David Jeremiah says, "He is the belt of truth, for He is the Way, the Truth and the Life. He is the breastplate, for He is our righteousness. He becomes our shoes of peace, because He is our peace. He is the shield of faith, for He is the author and finisher of our faith. And He is the helmet of salvation, for we are told in the Bible that we have the mind of Christ."[10]

So Christ is the key. Stay close to Jesus. As A. W. Tozer famously said, "The best way to keep the enemy out is to keep Christ in. . . . It is not the praying sheep Satan fears but the presence of the Shepherd."[11]

If we stay Christ-centered and Christ-focused and draw near to him each day, we will stand strong and will survive the spiritual onslaught arrayed against us.

CHAPTER 5

KEEP PUSHING

Prayer is simply the key to everything we need to do and be in
life. We must learn to pray. We have to. . . . There is nothing more
important, or harder, or richer, or more life-altering. . . . To fail to
pray, then, is not to merely break some religious rule—it is a failure
to treat God as God. It is a sin against his glory. . . . Prayer is simply
a recognition of the greatness of God.

TIM KELLER

Prayer is not overcoming God's reluctance; it is
laying hold of his highest willingness.

RICHARD TRENCH

RAY STEDMAN, WHO FOR MANY YEARS served as pastor of Peninsula Bible Church in Palo Alto, California, tells a story he heard from a retired mariner who navigated his ship through surging, stormy seas over a career of many years. This captain recounted weathering one especially wild storm where survival was by no means assured.

The old mariner said, "The Lord heard the voices of many strangers that night."[1]

I believe the same is true today. Perhaps in the midst of the peril and perplexity in today's world, you're turning to the Lord more often than ever before. In these times I think we all sense a need to take a knee in prayer like never before.

As we navigate these last days, few things are more important than our prayer lives. As S. D. Gordon once said, "You can do *more* than pray, *after* you have prayed. But you can *not* do more than pray *until* you have prayed."[2]

Jesus told his followers that their prayer lives must intensify as the days get darker. At the end of his great sermon about the end of days, Jesus said, "Keep alert at all times. And *pray* that you might be strong enough to escape these coming horrors and stand before the Son of Man" (Luke 21:36, emphasis added).

Right after his extensive instruction about the days before his coming in Luke 17, we read in Luke 18:1, "Jesus told his disciples a story to show that they should always pray and never give up." Jesus' follow-up to his teaching about the final days was a story about a desperate widow that highlights the need for persistent prayer. Jesus knew the challenges and cares of the end times must be met with persevering prayer.

Jesus' message is clear: just as the popular slogan said some time ago, we have to *PUSH*—Pray Until Something Happens.

We all sense a need to pray, and to keep praying, but if you're like me, you often feel woefully inadequate. Prayer is *essential*, but prayer is not easy. The great Scottish preacher Alexander Whyte once said, "If you want to humble a man, ask him about his prayer life."[3] That's true, isn't it? If we're honest, prayer is something we all struggle with, even (and perhaps especially) when times are uncertain. We know we need to pray, but sometimes we may secretly wonder if it really works.

Jesus' disciples experienced the same struggle with prayer in their day. The disciples never asked Jesus how to walk on water, how to still a storm, or how to do other miracles, but they did ask Jesus to teach them to pray (see Luke 11:1). We need the same help.

Other than regularly reading and meditating on the Bible, nothing is more essential to your spiritual life—and spiritual survival—than prayer. It's that simple. We need to learn to pray, and there's no better place to look than Luke 11:1-13. These verses provide answers from Jesus to three key questions about prayer:

> *What* are we to pray for? (verses 1-4)
> *How* are we to pray? (verses 5-10)
> *Why* are we to pray? (verses 11-13)

Our focus will be on the last two questions, but let's begin briefly with the most basic question—what should we pray to the Lord about?

WHAT TO PRAY

In response to the disciples' question, Jesus tells them what kinds of things to pray for. The prayer Jesus gives, commonly known as the Lord's Prayer, is shorter in Luke 11 than the version recorded in Matthew 6. They aren't exact, word-for-word copies, which means you don't have to pray these exact words. If the Lord wanted us to pray this prayer verbatim, the version in Luke 11 would be the same as the one in Matthew 6. However, while Jesus didn't give us this prayer to repeat over and over again, there's nothing wrong with using this prayer as long as it's not *routine* or *mechanical*. We should memorize it and cite it as we do other parts of Scripture.

Since the form of the model prayer in Matthew 6:9-13 is longer and more familiar than the one in Luke 11, let's look at that text in its traditional form as our guide.

> *Our Father who art in heaven,*
> *hallowed be thy name.*
> *Thy kingdom come.*
> *Thy will be done on earth, as it is in heaven.*
> *Give us this day our daily bread,*
> *and forgive us our trespasses,*
> *as we forgive those who trespass against us,*
> *and lead us not into temptation,*
> *but deliver us from evil.*

Before we get into the specifics, let's make a few general observations about this prayer.

It's a model prayer. It's a pattern, road map, or skeleton to guide our own praying. It's a sample of the main areas we're to cover in our daily prayers. As I've already stated, it's not a prayer for us to pray in some rote fashion, but a pattern or outline to follow.

It's not the "Lord's" prayer. While it's not wrong to call this the Lord's Prayer, it's more accurate and descriptive to call

> Pray to the Father about the family (our good: give *us*, forgive *us*, lead *us*)

The prayer moves from God's glory to our good. Notice the change in pronouns from "thy" ("your") to "our" and "us." Our focus and first priority in prayer is on God's glory. Then the model prayer brings us back to earth to pray for our own needs.

God has all the power, the majesty, and the glory; we have all the needs, wants, and poverty. He's got everything; we have nothing. Prayer is the ultimate act of dependence. As E. M. Bounds writes, "Prayer honors God; it dishonors self. It is man's plea of weakness, ignorance, want."[5]

With this overview, let's briefly look at the two divisions of this prayer and the six things we're to pray about.

Pray to the Father about the Father

The three requests in this first half of the prayer cover three areas:

> The Father's person: "hallowed be thy name"
> The Father's program: "thy kingdom come"
> The Father's priorities: "thy will be done"

"OUR FATHER, WHO ART IN HEAVEN"

The prayer begins with the one we seek in prayer—"Our Father." The word "Father" indicates *to whom* we pray, and the word "our" refers to *with whom* we pray. God is referred to as Father fourteen times in the Old Testament, yet always in reference to the nation of Israel, not individuals. Jesus calls God his Father more than sixty times in the Gospels. We have a new relationship with God. He is our Father through faith in Jesus.

When I think about God being my Father, my mind goes to my own dad. He's great at fixing things and working with his hands. He doesn't like talking on the phone, so when I call and my mom answers and I ask for him, my dad knows that I must need something. When he takes the phone, his first words are usually, "What do you need?" I like to think of my heavenly Father in the same way. When I come to him with my troubles and concerns as his child, his response is, "What do you need?"

The phrase "who art in heaven" references whom we're seeking. He resides in the heavens. He's seated on the throne. He is almighty, eternal, and infinite. God is near us—he's intimate. But he's also far beyond us—he's transcendent. First things first: before anything else, remember who it is you're praying to. Stop and think about the Father in the heavens before you go any further.

THE FATHER'S PERSON

The first request is that God's name be honored, revered, and set apart (that's what "hallowed" means). In ancient times, someone's name represented their person or nature— who they are. So this is a request that God be revered, set apart from everything else, and treated as holy. The Puritan

Thomas Watson noted that this is the one petition in this prayer that we will make for all eternity:

> When some of the other petitions shall be useless
> and out of date, as we shall not need to pray in
> heaven, "Give us our daily bread," because there
> shall be no hunger; nor, "Forgive us our trespasses,"
> because there shall be no sin; nor, "Lead us not into
> temptation," because the old serpent is not there
> to tempt: yet the hallowing of God's name will be
> of great use and request in heaven; we shall be ever
> singing hallelujahs, which is nothing else but the
> hallowing of God's name.[6]

This request is what the angels around the throne in heaven never cease to proclaim in Revelation 4:8—"Holy, holy, holy."

If we pray for God to make his name set apart, then it follows that we must pray and seek that *we* will be holy in our lives. The revering of God's name must begin in my life if I sincerely want to see it hallowed everywhere else. We should honestly ask ourselves, *Is God treated as holy in my life? My marriage? My family?*

THE FATHER'S PROGRAM

Next is "thy kingdom come." This is a longing for God's program to be fulfilled—for the weary, war-torn world we live in to be made right. When you think about it, all prayer is ultimately a cry for the Kingdom to come. When we pray about our fears and uncertainty, the nation and our leaders, temptation, family issues, financial concerns, or health problems, the final answer to every one of these issues of life is the arrival of Christ's Kingdom. The Kingdom is God's answer to all our cries, sighs, and whys. And when we ask for the Kingdom to come, for God's Kingdom to rule on earth, we implicitly pray that our lives will also be subject to him.

Haddon Robinson says, "We must be willing for all of the little kingdoms that matter so much to us now to be pulled down. If we want God's rule over all men and women at some future time, it follows that we will want His control in our lives today. Unless we are sufficiently concerned about making our lives His throne and bringing others into glad submission to Him, we cannot pray with integrity for His kingdom to come."[7]

It's been well said that when we pray "your kingdom *come*," we must pray "my kingdom *go*."

THE FATHER'S PRIORITIES

The final request in this first section of the prayer concerns God's will or priorities—"thy will be done on earth as it is in heaven." How is God's will done in heaven? Completely. Joyfully. Unceasingly. Perfectly. Immediately. This is an appeal for God's sovereignty to be manifested on earth.

Again, what we want for this world must first be true in our lives. We must abandon our will for his will and yield ourselves totally to him. The ultimate issue in our lives is lordship—who's in charge?

Pray to the Father about the Family

After we pray to the Father about the Father and his glory, we move to praying to the Father about the family and our good. Again, remember that all the pronouns here are plural. We pray for ourselves and others. It's difficult sometimes to avoid self-centered praying. We get so absorbed in our own needs, like the young woman who said, "Lord, I'm not going to pray for myself today; I'm going to pray for others," and after praying for some time, she added, "And give my mother a handsome son-in-law." Our prayers have a tendency to circle back to ourselves.

In the model prayer, Jesus focuses on three requests that we pray for ourselves and other believers.

OUR PROVISION

The first petition is "give us this day our daily bread." This is a humble request for provision. We ask God for what is needed for the day—*daily* bread. Each day brings its share of burdens and needs but also its joys and blessings.

Daily bread includes food but is not limited to that. Everything necessary for our body and our existence is captured in this request. Martin Luther helps us understand the full meaning of "daily bread":

> What does "Daily Bread" mean? Everything that
> nourishes our body and meets its needs, such as:
> Food, drink, clothing, shoes, house, yard, fields,
> cattle, money, possessions, a devout spouse, devout

THE END TIMES SURVIVAL GUIDE

children, devout employees, devout and faithful rulers, good government, good weather, peace, health, discipline, honor, good friends, faithful neighbors and other things like these.[8]

God is our Father. We can trust him to meet our daily needs. As Hudson Taylor reminds us,

It is not difficult for me to remember that the little ones need breakfast in the morning, dinner at midday, and something before they go to bed at night. Indeed, I could not forget it. And I find it impossible to suppose that our Heavenly Father is less tender or mindful than I. . . . I do not believe that our Heavenly Father will ever forget his children. I am a very poor father, but it is not my habit to forget my children. God is a very, very good Father. It is not his habit to forget his children.[9]

OUR PARDON

The second family request is for pardon from our sins. The model prayer Jesus gives us moves from "give" to "forgive"; from food to forgiveness.

The whole notion of forgiveness raises an important, practical question—if our debt is erased by God when we trust in Jesus and receive his forgiveness, why do we *still* need to ask for God's forgiveness? If all our debts have been paid and we have asked Jesus to forgive our sin once for all, why do we still need to be pardoned? (See Ephesians 1:7; Colossians 2:14.) It's easy to see why we need to ask God to forgive us once. Until we accept Christ's payment for our sins, we're not saved. I have to trust and believe that Jesus died on the cross to cancel my debt. Yet the prayer Jesus taught us in Matthew 6 makes asking for forgiveness part of our *daily* prayers. We ask for *daily pardon* as well as *daily provision*. But why do we need to keep asking for God's forgiveness? The answer is very simple—because we keep on sinning.

At this point, distinguishing two aspects of God's forgiveness is helpful.

1. *Final* forgiveness (relationship): This facet of our forgiveness brings us into an eternal relationship with our Father. Our sins are forever forgiven, blotted out, and removed far away (see Psalm 103:12; Jeremiah 31:34; Micah 7:19; Ephesians 1:7).

2. *Family* forgiveness (fellowship): Our daily sin interferes with our intimacy with our Father. It fractures our fellowship. As believers, we don't lose our relationship when we sin, but we do interrupt our fellowship with the Father. So we have to come daily for a fresh application of his forgiveness to maintain our fellowship with our Father. First John 1:9 says, "If we confess our sins to him, he is faithful and just to forgive us our sins and to cleanse us from all wickedness."

There's an old Dennis the Menace cartoon that pictures Dennis kneeling beside his bed at night, with hands clasped, eyes looking heavenward, saying, "Lord, I'm here to turn myself in." We have to come to God daily to turn ourselves in.

Jesus adds an interesting condition to our forgiveness: "As we forgive those who trespass against us." This is the only petition in this model prayer with a condition attached to it. The reason is because we sin *and* we are sinned against. We aren't the only ones in debt. We have debtors of our own: those who owe us something for what they've done to us. Our call when we are sinned against is to let it go. That's what forgiveness is. Forgiveness is a release, a letting go of destructive feelings like anger, bitterness, and revenge—attitudes that poison our lives. Forgiveness is not tolerating sin, excusing it, forgetting it, or covering it up. Forgiveness is letting it go. It's releasing the other person and also releasing ourselves from the burden of bitterness. Phil Ryken says,

> If we must forgive, then how shall we do it? What does it mean to forgive our debtors?
> It means to forgive everyone for everything. Forgive the neighbor who backed over your begonias. Forgive the sibling who colored in your books and the parent who never showed you very much affection. Forgive the spouse who doesn't meet your needs and the child who ran away from home. Forgive the coworker who stabbed you in the back and the boss who denied your promotion. Forgive

the church member who betrayed a confidence or the pastor who gave you poor spiritual care. Forgive people for whatever they have done to you.

If you are a Christian, you do not have the right to withhold forgiveness from anyone for anything.[10]

Jesus knew this would be the most difficult issue for his disciples and us to understand and apply, so he adds a postscript or appendix in Matthew 6:14-15: "If you forgive those who sin against you, your heavenly Father will forgive you. But if you refuse to forgive others, your Father will not forgive your sins."

This is not saying that our forgiveness merits God's forgiveness. It is saying that a mark of being forgiven is forgiving other people. Our forgiveness of others is evidence of our own forgiving spirit, and God only forgives the truly penitent. Refusing to forgive others is evidence that I myself am unforgiven.

The English poet George Herbert says, "He that cannot forgive others, breaks the bridge over which he himself must pass if he would ever reach heaven; for every one has need to be forgiven."[11] This doesn't mean that Christians never wrestle with forgiveness. But the struggle itself is evidence of God's grace in our hearts. And we may have to forgive over and over again. It can be a process, especially when the wounds are deep. At times, we may have to forgive all over again and continue to forgive as often as necessary. Like the rest of this prayer, forgiveness is part of everyday life for believers.

OUR PROTECTION

The final request in the model prayer ("lead us not into temptation but deliver us from evil") has probably caused more head-scratching than any other. The first thing to recognize is that this is not two separate requests but one petition in two parallel parts. "Lead us not into temptation" and "deliver us from evil" are two sides of the same request.

The main question in this request is why would we ask God not to lead us into temptation? Does God lead us into temptation? According to James 1:13, the answer is no. "When you are being tempted, do not say, 'God is tempting me.' God is never tempted to do wrong, and he never tempts anyone else."

So, what does Jesus mean in Matthew 6:13? The best explanation is that this is a figure of speech to express something positive by stating the opposite. "This is no small matter" means "This is a big matter." When we pray "lead us not into temptation," we're really praying "keep us away from temptation." "Don't let Satan ambush us." "Build a hedge around us." We need to ask the Lord, "If the opportunity to sin presents itself, please remove our desire. If the desire springs up within us, please don't allow us to have the opportunity."

HOW DO WE PRAY?

After telling us *what* to pray, Jesus tells a parable in Luke 11:5-10 that focuses on *how* we pray. His instruction is pointed: we're to pray persistently; we're not to give up. In our prayer life we must PUSH:

Then, teaching them more about prayer, he used this story: "Suppose you went to a friend's house at midnight, wanting to borrow three loaves of bread. You say to him, 'A friend of mine has just arrived for a visit, and I have nothing for him to eat.' And suppose he calls out from his bedroom, 'Don't bother me. The door is locked for the night, and my family and I are all in bed. I can't help you.' But I tell you this—though he won't do it for friendship's sake, if you keep knocking long enough, he will get up and give you whatever you need because of your shameless persistence."

LUKE 11:5-8

Jesus begins this story by drawing in the listener: "Suppose you went to a friend's house at midnight." The listener or reader is the person in need—that's *us*. We find ourselves in the story.

The parable revolves around a situation that could have arisen in ancient Near Eastern culture. An unexpected visitor arrives at midnight. This was quite common because people often traveled at night when it was cooler. The culture of the day demanded hospitality. It was a social duty and requirement. But the host has a problem: he has visitors and no food.

The cupboards are bare, and there are no 7-Eleven stores or twenty-four-hour Walmarts to shop at. The man is in a real bind. His only choice is to go next door to his neighbor in the dead of night.

To visualize this scene, we have to remember that families in that day lived in one-room houses. The entire family slept on one large mat on the floor. The animals were put to bed in another part of the room at night. The door to the house had a wooden or iron bar through rings in the door panels. Getting up and removing it would be noisy, and lighting a candle to find bread and rummaging through the kitchen would wake up the entire household. The situation presents a *massive* inconvenience, so the man responds, "Don't bother me. . . . I can't help you" (verse 7). Request denied!

The desperate neighbor does the only thing he can do: he knocks again and must have said something like, "Come on, man, you know I need some bread. I can't leave my visitors unfed. You have to help me!" You get the point: this man is not going away.

Jesus says, "If you keep knocking long enough, he will get up and give you whatever you need because of your shameless persistence" (verse 8). The word translated "shameless persistence" can also mean "gall," "nerve," or "bold perseverance."

We must be careful to note that God is not being compared to this tired, reluctant neighbor. Rather, he is being contrasted with him. What we have here is a "how much more" argument. Jesus is saying, "If even this unwilling neighbor will respond to persistence, how much more will our Father answer the persistent prayers of his people?" Our prayers are to be punctuated by commas, not periods.

Persistence in prayer is reinforced by Jesus' call in verses

9-10 to keep asking, keep seeking, and keep knocking. There's increasing intensity and a stacking of the words.

> Ask (prayer is asking for something)
> Seek (a stronger word than ask)
> Knock (relates back to the story of the man persistently knocking on the door)

God is ready to give, so *ask, seek,* and *knock.* PUSH—Pray Until Something Happens. As the Scottish theologian P. T. Forsyth writes, "Prayer is never rejected so long as we do not cease to pray. The chief failure of prayer is its cessation."[12]

This raises some important questions: Why does God want us to persist in prayer? Why does he sometimes delay his answers for so long? Why does God so often put us on hold? Why does he leave us waiting on the other end of the phone? What's the point? Do you ever feel like that? If God knows what we ask before we ask, if God hears us immediately, and if God is willing to answer us, why do we need to persist and persevere in prayer? Although much more could be said here about the mystery of prayer, here are five practical benefits of persistent prayer:

1. *Our faith is strengthened.* Our faith grows as we persist in seeking the Lord.
2. *We draw closer to the Lord.* Ben Patterson, in his book *Deepening Your Conversation with God,* says, "Perhaps one reason God delays his answers to our

prayers is because he knows we need to be with him far more than we need the things we ask of him."[13] Haddon Robinson says, "Those who are satisfied with the trinkets in the Father's hand miss the best reward of prayer—the reward of communicating and communing with the God of the universe."[14]

3. *Our patience is stretched.* We learn to wait on the Lord.

4. *Our gratitude grows.* That which is easily gained is often lightly appreciated. When we pray and seek the Lord for something over a period of time and the Lord answers our petition, we're filled with joy and thanksgiving.

5. *God may want to do something bigger.* God may delay his answer because he has something bigger in mind. I once heard someone, in reference to the story of the raising of Lazarus, say, "If Jesus had arrived on time he would have healed a sick man, but he waited a few days so He could raise a dead man." We have to persist in prayer and trust the Lord's timing, looking for the benefits his delays bring.

In these last days, as we face greater trials and opposition, we must not give up in our praying. No matter what—keep praying. Keep PUSHing.

WHY DO WE PRAY?

The final facet of Jesus' teaching on prayer in Luke 11 answers the "why" question. Why pray? The answer is simple: because of the nature of God. He is our Father. Our persistent prayer is rooted in the character of God as our Father.

> You fathers—if your children ask for a fish, do you give them a snake instead? Or if they ask for an egg, do you give them a scorpion? Of course not! So if you sinful people know how to give good gifts to your children, how much more will your heavenly Father give the Holy Spirit to those who ask him.
>
> LUKE 11:11-13

In verse 11, Jesus again draws in the listener—"You fathers—if your children ask for a fish . . ." Jesus is telling us we pray because God is our Father and is predisposed to give us good things, just as a father wants to bless his children. Jesus' teaching on prayer ends where it began, with the "Father" (Luke 11:2, 13). The word "Father" brackets the entire passage.

This gives us confidence and motivation to pray and to persist in prayer. The realization that our Father loves us and is willing to give us what is good should motivate us to persist in prayer. I love these words of Warren Wiersbe: "Prayer isn't bothering God, bargaining with God, borrowing from God, or burdening God. True prayer is blessing the Father because we love Him, trust Him, and know that He will meet our needs, so we come and ask."[15]

Our prayers get sifted through the goodness and wisdom of our Father. He will always and only give us what is good for us. Pray persistently, knowing that God is your loving Father who will only give you good gifts. If what you request is not best for you, God will not give it.

Dr. Howard Hendricks, a beloved professor for so many years at Dallas Theological Seminary, told of a time when he was a young man, before he was married. A certain mother in the church he attended came up to him one Sunday and said to him, "Howard, I just want you to know that I'm praying that you'll be my son-in-law." Dr. Hendricks, when telling this story, stopped at that point and said, very solemnly, "Have you ever thanked God for unanswered prayer?" I know I have.

We trust our Father to give us good gifts. But we don't receive just gifts; we receive the *Giver*. God gives us the Holy Spirit (see Luke 11:13). That's the greatest gift of all. He can't give more than himself.

As the world around us grows more chaotic and confusing, turn your panic into prayers. Don't be a stranger to God. Let him hear your voice often. Pray regularly. Pray repeatedly.

No matter what happens, keep PUSHing!

CHAPTER 6

DO THE BEST THINGS IN THE WORST TIMES

Never before in American history has it been more important for the church to be all that it can be in a society that is increasingly hostile to Christian values. . . . The darker the night, the more important every candle becomes.

ERWIN LUTZER

IN HIS BOOK *Shepherding the Church*, Joe Stowell records "an inspiring but little-known inscription hidden away in Harold Church, Staunton, England." The inscription is from 1653, and reflects a dark time for the Anglican Church in Great Britain. At the time, Oliver Cromwell was in power, and his mission was to remove any trace of the monarchy from the country. The Anglican Church thus came within his crosshairs since the head of that church was the king. As Stowell describes it, "Cromwell emptied the monasteries, removed baptismal fonts from the churches, defamed the clergy, and did everything in his power to disengage their place and influence in the culture. If you were an Anglican pastor, those were tough times to be in the religion business."

It is against this backdrop that the inscription from Harold Church was written: "In the year of 1653, when all things sacred were throughout the nation destroyed or profaned, this church was built to the glory of god by sir Robert Shirley, whose singular praise it was to have done the best things in the worst times."[1]

What a praise: doing "the best things in the worst times."

It certainly seems that we're living in the "worst times" for the United States spiritually, morally, and politically. Our nation is rapidly drifting away from God. Christianity is under attack from within and without. Biblical Christianity is in decline and vilified at every turn.

In these worst times, God is calling us to be about doing the best things. But what are the best things we must do? What activities and aspirations should capture our focus as time runs out?

No book in the New Testament answers this question more clearly than 1 Peter. The apostle Peter wrote this letter to believers scattered throughout central and northern Asia Minor (modern Turkey) in the early AD 60s. The audience Peter addressed was suffering persecution. The mistreatment was not empire-wide and did not involve physical suffering or martyrdom but consisted of mocking, slandering, maligning, and reviling (see 2:12; 3:16-17; 4:3-4, 14). The epistle 1 Peter was written to Jewish believers scattered throughout the Roman provinces of Asia Minor to encourage them in the face of localized persecution so that others could witness the true grace of God in their lives (see 5:12). In short, the purpose of 1 Peter is to show how to stand firm in God's grace in a hostile or Christian-unfriendly culture.

Peter develops several themes in his letter, but one thread that runs through the book is the coming of Jesus Christ. The return of Jesus serves as a kind of background music fostering hope and a sense of urgency to do the best things (see 1:7, 13; 2:12; 5:4). In hard times, God's people must stand firm. Peter believed the Lord could come at any moment and he motivates his readers to live in light of that day.

Peter's most detailed presentation of Christ's coming and how we should live in view of that reality is found in 4:7-11. There's no more simple, straightforward passage in the New Testament concerning what we should be doing if we believe Jesus is coming soon:

> The end of the world is coming soon. Therefore,
> be earnest and disciplined in your prayers. Most
> important of all, continue to show deep love for each
> other, for love covers a multitude of sins. Cheerfully
> share your home with those who need a meal or a
> place to stay. God has given each of you a gift from
> his great variety of spiritual gifts. Use them well to
> serve one another. Do you have the gift of speaking?
> Then speak as though God himself were speaking
> through you. Do you have the gift of helping others?
> Do it with all the strength and energy that God
> supplies. Then everything you do will bring glory to

THE END TIMES SURVIVAL GUIDE

God through Jesus Christ. All glory and power to
him forever and ever! Amen.

Verse 7 opens with the startling words, "The end of the
world is coming soon." Many wonder how Peter could say
that almost two thousand years ago. How could the end be
soon in the early AD 60s? Was Peter mistaken?

The consistent view of the early church was that Christ's
coming was near—that is, it could come at any moment
(see Romans 13:12; 1 Corinthians 7:29; Philippians 4:5;
Hebrews 10:25; James 5:8-9; Revelation 1:3; 22:20). Peter
pictures "the end as impending—having drawn near and
now in a position to break in at any time. . . . As human history moves alongside the edge of the eschatological future,
the line of separation at times seems razor-thin."[2]

Wayne Grudem states, "*The end of all things is at hand*
means that all the major events in God's plan of redemption
have occurred, and now all things are ready for Christ to
return and rule. . . . Thus the curtain could fall at any time."[3]

Daniel Segraves writes,

Since nothing else must occur before the event that
triggers all other eschatological events (the rapture
of the church), it is still correct to say, "The end
of all things is at hand." This is the doctrine of
imminence, which means that, so far as we know,
the end can come at any moment. It also means that,
as far as the writers of the New Testament knew, the
end could have come at any moment.[4]

When thinking about the arrival of the end, there's another aspect to this we should not overlook. None of us knows how near our own end is in the sense of personal, individual mortality.[5] None of us knows how much time we have personally or prophetically. We could encounter some tragedy and depart this world at any time. Prophetically, Jesus could come at any moment to catch his bride to heaven. In that sense, "the end of the world is coming soon." There's an ever-present "soonness" to the end of all things for all of us either way.

After reminding us that Christ could come at any moment, Peter's next word is "therefore." Peter is saying to us that since the Lord could return at any time, triggering the sequence of events that will bring history to a close, here's what we should be doing. Knowing should fuel a sense of urgency and simplicity.

When speaking of the Lord's return, not all believers agree on the details, but we can all agree on the demands of the experience.[6] First Peter 4:7-11 outlines four things we should do if we believe that the Lord is coming soon. We could call these the "Peter Principles" of spiritual survival in the last days, the best things we can do in the worst of times.

KEEP YOUR HEAD CLEAR: PRAY

The end of the world is coming soon. Therefore, be earnest and disciplined in your prayers.

I PETER 4:7

Peter's first principle is for believers to stay calm and balanced in order to have a devoted prayer life. After saying, "The end of the world is coming soon," Peter follows immediately by calling us to be "earnest" and "disciplined." He knows that in light of end-times events, many people are prone to get unbalanced and go to extremes.

We see this today. As things in the world continue to spiral out of control, some people can't resist the temptation to get caught up in all kinds of prophetic foolishness and frenzy, which is not conducive to a rich prayer life. The most egregious form of prophetic hysteria is date-setting for the coming of Christ or the end of the world. A charismatic leader will claim to know when Jesus is returning to earth, and in extreme examples, followers may even liquidate their possessions to prepare. The last two centuries are littered with failed predictions, disgraced "prophets," and disappointed followers.

What's amazing is that Jesus claimed during his earthly ministry that even he did not know the day of his coming (see Matthew 24:36). Anyone who claims to know the specific time of Christ's coming is claiming to know something the Father didn't tell even the Son while he was on earth. This is the height of arrogance and folly.

A biblical approach to the end times will never promote panic or frantic activity. The New Testament knows nothing of apocalyptic hysteria. Rather, in view of the end of all things, believers are to be "earnest" and "disciplined." Being earnest means being sensible, prudent, balanced, and proportionate in our reactions and possessing a clear mind.

The word *disciplined* means literally "sober" or "not drunk." In other words, we are to be sober-minded, clearheaded, and mentally alert for the purpose of prayer. We are to be earnest and disciplined so that we are disposed to pray. Believing that the end of all things is at hand should spur us on to a disciplined prayer life. When we're sane and sober, we can pray more effectively and appropriately, and as the troubles of the last days increase, prayer is more important than ever. As we await the end of all things, we're to pray, not panic.

In our present day, prayer is needed on every front—individually and corporately in our families, churches, and society. Perilous times must be faced with prayer. Nothing else will do.

As Charles Swindoll notes, "When something alarms you, pray. When current events confuse you, pray. If the world looks like it's spinning out of control, pray. In fact, prayer is what sharpens our awareness so that we are able to be more discerning. It gives us genuine hope and confidence in Christ in the midst of confusion. When you're panicking, you're not praying."[7]

To survive spiritually, don't get caught up in end-times hysteria.

Don't panic; pray.

KEEP YOUR HEART WARM: LOVE

Most important of all, continue to show deep love for each other, for love covers a multitude of sins.

I PETER 4:8

According to Jesus, one of the signs of the Second Coming is that "the love of many will grow cold" (Matthew 24:12). Paul reminded Timothy that in the last days, "people will love only themselves" (2 Timothy 3:2). The final days will be marked by lack of love, and more and more our world is descending into the cold, hateful place predicted in Scripture.

In contrast, the badge of Christianity is love (see John 13:34-35). As we see the end approaching, Peter reminds us that believers are to be marked by a "deep love" for one another. The word translated "deep" was used in ancient times of a horse at full gallop when its muscles were stretched to the limit. Peter is saying that our love for one another is to be stretched out to the limits but never reaching its breaking point. Our love for our fellow believers is to keep "stretching, in both depth and endurance."[8]

First Peter 4:8 focuses on our love for one another as believers, but I believe it's valid to extend this command outward to the world around us. As our world becomes colder and more callous, believers should be a haven of warmth and winsomeness. Yet sadly, many believers are responding to the world's hostility in kind. Erwin Lutzer challenges this attitude: "We are not a majority, but God keep us from becoming an angry, vindictive minority! Self-pity loses sight of the promises of God and leads to a mindset of withdrawal, an attitude that says, 'Since they hate us, let them rot.' How unlike our Master!"[9]

A reason for or result of loving others is included: "For love covers a multitude of sins." Love doesn't *condone* sin, but it does *cover* it. When we love others, we will be gentle with their weaknesses and failures and won't broadcast their sin to humiliate or injure them. We should derive no delight from finding and exposing the faults and sins of others.

KEEP YOUR HOME OPEN: SHARE

> Cheerfully share your home with those who need a meal or a place to stay.
>
> 1 PETER 4:9

As love is in short supply in these last days, the love of believers must increase and intensify. One concrete expression of love is reaching out in hospitality to strangers. Hospitality is a specific aspect or subset of love.

The beautiful Christian virtue of hospitality is mentioned repeatedly in the New Testament (see Romans 12:13; 1 Timothy 3:2; 5:9-10; Titus 1:8; Hebrews 13:1-3; 3 John 1:5-8). As this world becomes a colder and more isolating place, we are to keep our homes open and show the warmth of Christ to strangers.

With the influx of immigrants and refugees into the United States and other nations, it's common to hear people speak of those who oppose unrestrained immigration as *xenophobic*, which means a fear of strangers. This slur is the opposite of what Peter references by his use of the word *philoxenos*, which means to love or befriend strangers. Believers are to have an affectionate concern for strangers always but even more in light of the any-moment coming of Christ. Max Lucado underscores the simplicity and impact of hospitality:

Something holy happens around a dinner table that will never happen in a sanctuary. In a church auditorium you see the backs of heads. Around the table you see the expressions on faces. In the auditorium one person speaks; around the table everyone has a voice. Church services are on the clock. Around the table there is time to talk.

Hospitality opens the door to uncommon community. . . . When you open your door to someone, you are sending this message: "You matter to me and to God." You may think you are saying, "Come over for a visit." But what your guest hears is, "I'm worth the effort."[10]

Hospitality is simple yet sublime. It's something almost every believer can do, yet as our society becomes more disconnected and distracted, it's becoming more and more rare.

There's an important condition added to our hospitality. It must be expressed "cheerfully," not with grumbling or complaining. We all know that showing hospitality can be costly in both money and time. It can be messy, inconvenient, and occasionally frustrating. When extending hospitality, God's people need to display a positive, cheerful attitude.

I like the story of a poor, tired, hungry traveler, walking a country road in England, who came to an inn bearing the name "George and the Dragon." The man knocked on the door.

"Is there any food I can have?" the man asked when he

saw a woman's head pop out of a window to see who was at the door.

The woman saw his shabby clothes and knew he probably wouldn't be able to pay. "No!" she practically yelled.

"Can you spare some ale?"

"No!" she said again.

"That's all right. But is there any room in your stable for me to rest?"

"No!"

The traveler thought a moment before speaking again. "Is George around? Could I have a word with him instead?"[11]

In these times, as our world becomes a colder, less inviting place, we each need to take stock and honestly ask ourselves, *When it comes to showing hospitality to strangers, am I George . . . or the dragon? Am I willing to move outside my comfort zone to befriend and bless strangers the Lord brings across my path?*

KEEP YOUR HANDS BUSY: SERVE

God has given each of you a gift from his great variety of spiritual gifts. Use them well to serve one another. Do you have the gift of speaking? Then speak as though God himself were speaking through you. Do you have the gift of helping others? Do it with all the strength and energy that God supplies. Then everything you do will bring glory to God through Jesus Christ. All glory and power to him forever and ever! Amen.

I PETER 4:10-11

Jesus gave his disciples specific, final instructions about how they were to use their gifts, talents, and possessions in his absence in the form of a parable found in Matthew 25:14-30. Jesus told a similar parable in Luke 19. There a nobleman entrusts his possessions to his servants before he embarks on a long trip and leaves them with these final instructions: "Invest this for me while I am gone" (Luke 19:13). The King James Version translates this, "Occupy till I come." Jesus is saying we must maximize the abilities, gifts, and opportunities he gives us while we wait for him to return. Our instructions are clear: keep your hands busy.

Every believer in Jesus Christ has at least one spiritual gift given to us by the Master to use in his service. No believer has all the gifts, and a believer can have more than one gift, but there is no such thing as an ungifted believer.

A spiritual gift is a skill or ability given by God for regular use to perform a function in the body of Christ with ease and effectiveness. More simply, a spiritual gift is a God-given ability for Christian service. (For a list of spiritual gifts, see Romans 12:6-8; 1 Corinthians 12:8-11, 28-31; Ephesians 4:11.)

Many wonder what the difference is between a natural talent or ability and a spiritual gift. One distinction is that natural talent comes by natural birth, whereas spiritual gifts come by new birth. Having said that, the two are not always easy to distinguish in their expression because natural talents and skills are also from God. They are clearly different, but they often complement each other. God in his providence knew he was going to save us and gave us natural talents at birth that can be enhanced by our spiritual gifts at our new birth.

9 Key Truths about Spiritual Gifts

1. Every believer has a spiritual gift or gifts.

2. A gift is received at the moment of salvation.

3. A gift is a divine enablement that manifests God's grace.

4. It's to be used to serve others.

5. It's a stewardship.

6. There is great variety in spiritual gifts.

7. There are two basic categories of gifts: speaking gifts and serving gifts.

8. We must depend on God in the use of gifts.

9. The ultimate purpose of these gifts is to glorify God.

One benefit of knowing your spiritual gift is that it helps you to know where to focus your time and effort for the greatest impact in God's service. So, how can you discover your spiritual gift? Let me suggest five simple steps.

First, there are two broad categories of gifts: speaking gifts and serving gifts. Begin by determining which broad category your gifting falls in; then read the New Testament gift lists to get more specific.

Second, pray for the Lord's guidance. He wants you to discover your gift and use it more than you do.

THE END TIMES SURVIVAL GUIDE

Third, don't make this overly complicated. Begin to do something and trust God to lead you into your sweet spot of spiritual service. We discover by doing. That's the same way we discover our natural talents for things such as sports or music. As the old saying goes, "It's hard to steer a parked car."

Fourth, as you begin to serve or speak, listen to the input and evaluation of others. They serve as a valuable, objective resource and sounding board.

I like the story of a young farmer who was out plowing in his field one day. He stopped for a rest, wiped the perspiration from his brow, and looked up into the sky. The clouds had formed two letters—PC. "That's it!" he exclaimed. "Preach Christ! The Lord is telling me to preach Christ!"

He went to several churches in the area and tried to speak, but his messages weren't well delivered and didn't inspire or encourage the congregation. Finally, an old deacon called him aside and said, "Son, what makes you think you've been called to preach?"

The man said, "I saw it written in the clouds. PC—Preach Christ."

The deacon said, "Son, I think you missed it. I believe the Lord was telling you to *plant corn*."[12]

Others can help you in discerning God's calling and gifting. When you're functioning in the area of your gift, others will take note of it and ask you to do it and enjoy watching you do it.

Fifth, think about what you enjoy and what you do with

ease and effectiveness. When you use your gift, you will enjoy it, which means you're probably on the right track. When you use your gift, you will be fulfilled, and you won't be totally fulfilled unless and until you use it.

Ray Stedman summarizes:

> Now we close with this question: Who are you, anyway? Every morning you ought to ask yourself that. Who am I? And your answer should come from the Scriptures: I am a son of God among the sons of men. I am equipped with the power of God to labor today. At the very work that is given to me today God will be with me, doing it through me. I am gifted with special abilities to help people in various areas, and I don't have to wait until Sunday to start to utilize these gifts: I can do it at my work, I can do it anywhere. I can exercise the gift that God has given me to do. As soon as I begin to find out what it is, by taking note of my desires, and by asking others what they see in me, and by trying out various things, I am going to set myself to the lifelong task of keeping that gift busy.[13]

God supplies the strength we need to exercise our gifts whether they involve speaking or serving. His supply is limitless to enable and energize us.

My friend Pastor Philip De Courcy lives in California but was born and raised in Belfast, Northern Ireland. When he and his wife and three daughters were on their way to the ceremony to become US citizens, Philip was feeling patriotic and asked them what they liked best about America. Philip went first and waxed eloquent about the freedom Americans enjoy. As others were thinking about their answer, from the back seat one of his daughters said, "My favorite thing about America is free refills."

If you've ever been to Europe, that answer makes sense. Over there, when you order a soft drink, it's expensive, and you have to pay for every refill. For a young person, what could be better than free refills? And for a believer, what could be better than a God who gives free refills of his grace and strength? His power can never be diminished or exhausted. He is always available, and his help is unlimited.

A doxology closes the passage above—"All glory and power to him forever and ever! Amen." (1 Peter 4:11)—reminding us that in all our service, we get no glory. All the glory goes to the Lord.

Corrie ten Boom was a wonderful model of this idea of God receiving all the glory. Although she received notoriety during her lifetime, she said of her own position, "When Jesus rode into Jerusalem on Palm Sunday on the back of a donkey, and everyone was waving palm branches and throwing garments on the road, and singing praises, do you think that for one moment it ever entered the head of that donkey that any of that was for him? If I can be the donkey on which Jesus Christ rides in His glory, I give him all the praise and all the honor."[14]

THE END

In light of the end of all things, God doesn't call us to acts of fanaticism or hysteria, and he doesn't necessarily call us to heroic feats of bravery or courage. The actions in 1 Peter 4:7-11 are simple things we can all do every day.

"The end of the world is coming soon," Peter writes. "Therefore . . ."

> Keep your head clear.
> Keep your heart warm.
> Keep your home open.
> Keep your hands busy.

These are the best things we can do in the worst times. These are things we can all do every day.

And never forget to give God all the glory.

CHAPTER 7

FIND YOUR FRAIDY HOLE

We cannot talk about standing on the Rock of Ages and then act as if we are clinging to our last piece of driftwood.

ANONYMOUS

Do you remember the movie *Twister*? It's one of my all-time favorite movies—not because I enjoy disasters but because I live in Oklahoma, where, unfortunately, tornadoes are a part of life. I've lived here for all but three years of my life, so I've seen hundreds of tornado watches and warnings, heard the haunting blare of warning sirens, and seen my share of funnels in person and from storm chasers' videos. Central and northern Oklahoma are part of a region that has been dubbed "Tornado Alley." Oklahoma is known for three things: football, oil, and tornadoes.

Tornadoes are such a part of Oklahoma life and culture that most homes have what has come to be known as a "fraidy hole" or an underground storm shelter. "Fraidy hole" is an appropriate name because few things are more frightening than a tornado—the dark, ominous skies; the wall cloud; the spinning funnel; the debris cloud. When new families move to Oklahoma, it's not unusual for them to experience serious anxiety and even panic when the first tornado watches and warnings are issued.

None of the houses my wife and I had lived in since we'd been married had a storm shelter, so when we built our current home, one nonnegotiable feature was a fraidy hole. A home without a shelter was not an option.

Meteorologists in Oklahoma urge everyone to have a safe place to hide in the event a twister comes calling. Every spring, when tornado season ramps up and twisters spin across the landscape, local meteorologists track tornadoes, calling on those in the storm path to go to their designated safe places. Our new safe place is the fraidy hole underneath the floor in our garage. It's very snug, but it's safe. We've already used it once. And my wife loves it.

As the storm clouds gather and our world spins out of control, we all sense the need to have a spiritual fraidy hole or shelter where we can retreat to ride out the storms. Jesus highlighted the sweeping fear that will mark the end times:

> You will hear of wars and threats of wars, but don't panic.
>
> MATTHEW 24:6

> People will be terrified at what they see coming upon the earth.
>
> LUKE 21:26

In these distressing days, we need a safe place away from the panic. We need a refuge. I can't think of a better spiritual fraidy hole than another famous "46 defense," Psalm 46:

> God is our refuge and strength,
> A very present help in trouble.
> Therefore we will not fear, though the earth should
>   change
> And though the mountains slip into the heart of the sea;
> Though its waters roar and foam,
> Though the mountains quake at its swelling pride.
>   *Selah.*

> There is a river whose streams make glad the city of God,
> The holy dwelling places of the Most High.
> God is in the midst of her, she will not be moved;
> God will help her when morning dawns.
> The nations made an uproar, the kingdoms tottered;
> He raised His voice, the earth melted.
> The LORD of hosts is with us;
> The God of Jacob is our stronghold.   *Selah.*

> Come, behold the works of the LORD,
> Who has wrought desolations in the earth.
> He makes wars to cease to the end of the earth;
> He breaks the bow and cuts the spear in two;
> He burns the chariots with fire.
> "Cease striving and know that I am God;

> I will be exalted among the nations, I will be exalted in
> the earth."
> The LORD of hosts is with us;
> The God of Jacob is our stronghold.   *Selah.* (NASB)

THE 9/11 PSALM

The terrorist attack on September 11, 2001, was an American tragedy. The surprise attack against America shook us to the core individually and nationally. We were left reeling. The stunning images of that day still arouse deep feelings in all our hearts. The day after 9/11 I was at Dallas Theological Seminary, and the sorrow was palpable. An unusually sober, solemn atmosphere hung over the campus. As we were going into chapel, I overheard someone ask the venerable professor Dr. J. Dwight Pentecost what he was thinking about in light of all the recent events. I'll never forget his reply. All he said was "Psalm 46, Psalm 46." His response has stayed with me all these years.

Then, at the National Prayer Service on Friday, September 14, Billy Graham offered words of comfort to the families of the fallen, the survivors, and the entire nation. During his comments, he read Psalm 46. Those words struck a chord.

I remember turning to Psalm 46 several times that week in 2001, and I found peace, security, and calm.

The great reformer Martin Luther faced numerous dangers and threats on his life from the pope and his forces in the sixteenth century. At one point he spent eleven months in hiding at Wartburg Castle. In the face of opposition, excommunication, and pressure from every side to back down, he stood firmly for the truth of salvation by God's grace through faith alone. Luther's favorite Bible passage was Psalm 46. The words of that psalm inspired him to write his triumphant hymn "A Mighty Fortress Is Our God." When Luther became fearful, discouraged, or insecure, he would say to his friend and coworker Philipp Melanchthon, "Come, Philipp, let us sing the Forty-Sixth Psalm," and they would lift their voices to God in praise.[1]

When I feel insecure or afraid, I often find myself turning to Psalm 46 as well. It's the divine fraidy hole when the twisters of life are spinning out of control. With all that's going on in our world today as the end of the age closes in, my time in Psalm 46 has become more frequent. As we move deeper into the last days, perilous times will increase in frequency and intensity.

Added to the mounting international, global concerns are our fears about our own lives that can make cowards even of the best of us. Ann Landers was a popular syndicated advice columnist. At one time she was receiving ten thousand letters a month from people with all kinds of problems. "Someone asked her if there was one common denominator among all her correspondents. She said that the great overriding theme of all the letters she read was *fear*—fear of nearly everything imaginable until the problem became, for countless readers, a fear of life itself."[2]

I've been there; so have you. How can we feel secure in a world filled with insecurity?

The answer today to our fears and insecurity is the same as it was in Martin Luther's day and the same as it was on 9/11—Psalm 46. We all need a huge dose of Psalm 46. It can be our fraidy hole in these stormy times.

I like the story about the little boy who was afraid of the dark. One night his mother told him to fetch the broom that was out on the back porch. "Mama, it's dark out there," the little boy said. "You know I'm afraid of the dark."

His mother responded, "Jesus is out there, so you don't have to be afraid. He'll protect you."

The little boy asked, "Are you sure he's out there?"

"Yes, I'm sure," the mother said. "He is everywhere."

The little boy thought about that and then cracked the door open. He called out, "Jesus? If you're out there, would you please hand me the broom?"

Just like that little boy, our security in the darkness comes from knowing God is with us. Security is found in God's presence. That's the simple, strong message of Psalm 46—the answer to panic and peril is the presence of God.

God's presence as the source of our security is highlighted repeatedly in Psalm 46 (see verses 1, 5, 7, 11). The only safe, secure place in these last days is in knowing God is with us. God's presence is our fraidy hole.

GETTING OUR BEARINGS

Before we begin to unpack Psalm 46, we need to think for a few moments about the background of this psalm. We can't be sure about its historical setting, but many believe it's from the days of Hezekiah, one of the kings of Judah. In 701 BC, the Assyrian king Sennacherib was leading his army on a ruthless march through the Mediterranean world. Twenty years earlier Sennacherib's predecessor had stormed the northern kingdom of Israel's capital, Samaria, and deported the ten northern tribes, depopulating the nation. Once again, like a swarm of locusts, they descended on the tiny nation of Judah, conquering and consuming everything in their path. Sennacherib marched through Judah in 701 BC with a massive army of almost two hundred thousand.

By the time he got to Jerusalem, more than two hundred thousand Jews had been taken captive, along with much spoil. Forty-six cities had fallen. Sennacherib besieged Jerusalem, and it was only a matter of time before the city would fall. The Assyrians engaged in psychological warfare, sending messengers outside the walls of the city to taunt the people and their God in an effort to persuade them to surrender. As you can imagine, the city was gripped with crippling fear. This was a 9/11 scenario for Judah.

The Assyrian king sent a letter to King Hezekiah mocking God and urging him to surrender. I love the words of 2 Kings 19:14: "After Hezekiah received the letter from the messengers and read it, he went up to the LORD's Temple and spread it out before the LORD." Hezekiah spread the letter out before the Lord as if to say, "Read this, Lord. Look at what I'm facing. Help me." Hezekiah did what we must do in times of trouble. He turned panic into prayer. He laid it all out before the Lord and left it all in God's hands.

In 2 Kings 19:35, we read, "Then it happened that night that the angel of the LORD went out and struck 185,000 in the camp of the Assyrians; and when men rose early in the morning, behold, all of them were dead" (NASB). Did you catch the words "that night"? The very night when Hezekiah prayed, the Lord intervened dramatically. A lone angelic warrior dispatched from heaven destroyed the Assyrian juggernaut. The citizens of Jerusalem woke up the next morning to a killing field littered with almost two hundred thousand corpses. Proud King Sennacherib retreated to Nineveh in total humiliation. He was sent packing. Back in Nineveh he was later assassinated by his own sons.

One interesting historical footnote confirms that something dramatic happened to the Assyrian army in Judah. The Taylor Prism, a hexagonal clay document in the British Museum, contains Sennacherib's account of the siege of Jerusalem in 701 BC. In his chronicle, Sennacherib never explains why he failed to conquer Jerusalem, capture its king, and annex Judah as part of his kingdom. The Assyrian military machine that steamrolled everything in its path inexplicably failed to subdue the tiny nation of Judah and its capital city, Jerusalem.

The reason for Sennacherib's epic failure? The destroying angel.

It is thought that Psalm 46 commemorates this deliverance. It's a psalm of trust or confidence. The divine deliverance of Judah in Hezekiah's day serves as a foretaste or preview of what God will do when he finally defeats all his enemies and ushers in his kingdom of peace (verse 9). That's the day we anticipate.

There are three movements, stanzas, or natural breaks in the Psalm, each ending with the word *Selah* (probably a musical notation denoting a pause). Each stanza addresses a different situation with a corresponding reaction rising from faith:

Situation 1: Nature, in upheaval.
Reaction: I will not fear. (vv. 2–3)
Selah!

Situation 2: Jerusalem, under attack.
Reaction: I will not be moved. (vv. 4–7)
Selah!

Situation 3: Battlefield, after war.
Reaction: I will not strive. (vv. 8–11)
Selah![3]

The threefold outline we will use is simple:

> Our Refuge (verses 1-3)
> Our River (verses 4-7)
> Our Ruler (verses 8-11)

OUR REFUGE

The Lord is "our refuge and strength" in times of trouble. He is our hiding place. He is our fraidy hole.

The word "trouble" in Psalm 46:1 refers to a tight place or tight spot. It's when you feel like you're painted into a corner. King Hezekiah and Judah were certainly in a jam in the events that are believed to have given rise to this psalm. From the Taylor Prism, we know Sennacherib boasted that he had Hezekiah "shut up like a bird in a cage" in the city of Jerusalem. Hezekiah was trapped. The siege encircling the city was airtight. Yet God was with Hezekiah, and he's with us, too, if we know him. God is our refuge, our security, our hiding place. He's our strength who helps us. The Lord hides us and helps us when we find ourselves in the tight places and traps of life—when we face our own Sennacheribs.

But we must remember that God doesn't hide us and help us to take us out of the fray but only to protect and strengthen us for a time until we can get back into action. Warren Wiersbe says it well: "He hides us that He might help us, and then He thrusts us back into the battle that we might accomplish His will in this world. God does not hide us to pamper us, but to prepare us, He strengthens us that He might use us."[4] That's an important reminder.

The truths in Psalm 46 are real no matter how bad it gets. The word "though" occurs four times in the psalm in the New American Standard Bible, each time highlighting in poetic language some devastating national peril or cataclysm:

> > "*though* the earth should change": nothing is more stable and predictable than the earth's landscape; only extreme conditions can alter it.

> "*though* the mountains slip into the heart of the sea":
nothing is more immovable than a mountain.
> "*though* its waters roar and foam," "*though* the
mountains quake at its swelling pride": the oceans
threaten to overwhelm the mountains.

These four phrases symbolize an unimaginable, threatening doomsday scenario. Using highly charged, symbolic language, the psalmist is saying, "No matter how bad it gets, we have a refuge," even if a spiritual F-5 tornado is bearing down on us.

How can the psalmist say that in the face of such peril and upheaval? How can we? Because we have one who hides us and helps us.

There's a great story from the life of Frederick Nolan, who served as a missionary in North Africa. Nolan was trying to get away from his enemies during a time of persecution, and hiding places were scarce. Eventually, he was so weary that he had to give up running and take refuge in a small cave, fully expecting that his enemies would find him. While he waited for his enemies to arrive, he watched with fascination as a spider began to spin a web over the entrance of the cave. It started small, but in just a few minutes, the web covered the entire entrance of the cave. Nolan's enemies came just as he had expected, but after some deliberation, they passed on. There's no way that Nolan could be in the cave, they reasoned, because he would have had to break the spider's web to get in. Nolan escaped and later wrote about this incident,

"Where God is, a spider's web is like a wall. Where God is not, a wall is like a spider's web."[5]

As Proverbs 18:10 reminds us, "The name of the LORD is a strong fortress; the godly run to him and are safe." When all else is moving, we go to the one who is immovable. When everything is shifting, we go to the one who is secure. As Erwin Lutzer says, "We must cling to what is unmovable in an age when everything that has been nailed down is being torn up."[6]

Vance Havner told a story about an elderly woman who was greatly disturbed by her many troubles, both real and imaginary, and visited every doctor in town. Finally, someone in her family tactfully told her, "Grandma, we've done all we can for you. You'll just have to trust God for the rest." A look of absolute despair spread over her face as she replied, "Oh dear, has it come to that?" Havner wisely commented, "It always comes to that, so we might as well begin with that!" It *does* always come to that for all of us. We must trust God as our refuge and strength.

There's a comforting truth here about God and his help. Psalm 46:1 says God is "a very present help" (NASB). The New Living Translation says that God is "always ready to help in times of trouble." He's not just a help; he's *always* present to help us.

This means:

> God is always available.
> God is instantly present in any situation.

> God is easy to find.
> God is accessible.

Psalm 46:5 alludes to the destruction of the Assyrian army: "God will help her when morning dawns" (NASB). The King James Version translates it, "God shall help her, and that right early." Or as we would say, "in the nick of time."

Remember, when Hezekiah prayed while the Assyrian army was camped outside Jerusalem, 2 Kings 19:35 says "that night" God sent his angel to wipe out the Assyrian army. God's help was in the nick of time. It was available. Of course, not every cry to God is met with an immediate response, but the point is that God's help is timely. He is always right on time, even if his timetable is not our timetable.

The people of Judah woke up in the morning, and God had miraculously delivered them from the Assyrians. I'm sure you've gone to bed sometime, burdened and distressed about some difficulty you were facing, only to awake in the morning to discover that God had sorted it all out while you slept. His help is timely.

Several years ago I had the privilege to speak at Harvest Christian Fellowship in Riverside, California, where Greg Laurie pastors. We were sitting in his office chatting when his granddaughter came into his office, and Pastor Laurie handed her a small toy. I could tell he couldn't wait to give it to her. She was so happy, but it quickly became clear that the toy wasn't working. She asked him if he could fix it, and he immediately took it from her and began working on it. He worked and worked on it to no avail. He was undeterred. We continued to talk, but his focus was on that little, inexpensive toy. I was pleased and even amused to see this well-known pastor spending thirty minutes tediously working on a flimsy toy that wouldn't last but a few days. Yet his granddaughter had a need, so he was immediately available for her. He was instantly accessible to help with the problem. And finally, he got it to work. I think he was happier about it than his granddaughter was.

God is like that for his children. He's accessible when we need help. He *wants* to help us.

Far too many believers see God as far off, inaccessible, and maybe even uninterested in what's happening to them. The psalmist tells us God is a refuge that's approachable and easy to find.

When peril raises its head, go to your fraidy hole, your safe place, your refuge—find your Father. As Isaiah 41:10 says, "Don't be afraid, for I am with you."

OUR RIVER

The middle stanza of Psalm 46 references a river: "There is a river whose streams make glad the city of God" (verse 4, NASB). This center stanza presents a striking contrast between the raging waters and foaming oceans that rattle us (verses 1-3) and the calm, flowing river that refreshes us (verses 4-7).

Most great cities of the world are situated on or near a river. Paris has the Seine. London, the Thames. Washington, DC, the Potomac. New York City, the Hudson. Tokyo, the

Sumida. Vienna, the Danube. The reference to the city of God in Psalm 46 is clearly Jerusalem, which is interesting, because Jerusalem has no natural water source. It's one of the few major ancient cities not built on a river, which left it in a precarious position. Without a water supply within or alongside the city, if it was besieged, the people were finished.

Anticipating the Assyrian invasion and siege, Hezekiah wisely cut an underground tunnel to bring water from the Gihon Spring outside the city into the Pool of Siloam and then from there underneath the city through a tunnel into a repository. This left no water on the outside for the Assyrians while providing Jerusalem with its own underground river inside the walls of the city.

The tunnel Hezekiah dug, which is still around today, is over 1,700 feet long, hewn out of solid rock. Known today as Hezekiah's Tunnel, this marvelous feat of engineering was dug from each end, meeting in the middle. The water or river it channeled into the city was the water supply that provided for the inhabitants of Jerusalem during the siege.

That water source is used by the psalmist as a picture of the greater spiritual resource of the Lord himself for his people. What the tunnel and water supply were physically to the people, God is spiritually. Everything that a river is to a city, God is to his people. He's the fountain of life, the source of refreshment and joy. As Robert J. Morgan says,

> Think of it. On the surface, there was no water. No river. No refreshment. No life-giving currents. Outside

the city, an amassed army. But deep below the level
of the streets and homes, beneath the ground level of
ancient Jerusalem, there was a hidden river coursing
through the rocks. There was a secret spring, a reliable
source of water to refresh the trapped inhabitants
who, though besieged, were assured of victory. . . .

There's spiritual meaning here. Far beneath the
ground level of life, below our homes and streets
and everyday activities, there is a secret spring for
Christians—a reliable source of refreshment the
enemy cannot figure out, and whose flow cannot be
interrupted.[7]

God is our Refuge, so we need not fear.
God is also our River, so we need not faint.

OUR RULER

The final stanza of Psalm 46 underscores the sovereignty of
God. In these verses two main points surface.

Behold His Works

Psalm 46:8-9 brings us to the end of history, long after the
Assyrian army has been wiped out. In these verses the Prince
of Peace has been enthroned on earth. This looks ahead to
the future, messianic kingdom of Jesus on earth:

Come, behold the works of the LORD,
Who has wrought desolations in the earth.

He makes wars to cease to the end of the earth;
He breaks the bow and cuts the spear in two;
He burns the chariots with fire.

PSALM 46:8-9, NASB

This passage has never been fulfilled at any time in the past and will only be fulfilled when Jesus comes back to earth someday to crush his foes, bring an end to human warfare, and establish his kingdom on earth (see Revelation 19:11–20:6). As Charles Swindoll says,

> The songwriter now surveys a battlefield. He invites
> us to view the mute reminders of war, a terrain
> littered with bodies and debris. Chariots lie on their
> sides, burned, and now rusty. Dust and debris cover
> broken bows and splintered spears. War itself has been
> decimated. The song describes a scene not unlike the
> aftermath of World War II. The beaches of Normandy;
> the cities of Berlin and Hiroshima; sections of London;
> the islands of Iwo Jima, Guadalcanal, and Okinawa.
> Rusty tanks. Sunken boats covered with barnacles.
> Concrete bunkers. A silence pervades. It is as though
> our God has said, "That is enough!" When the Lord
> acts, He's thorough.[8]

At this point, all the tumult and cataclysm will cease. Man's day will end. The sovereign Messiah will reign over all the earth.

Bow to His Ways

Psalm 46:10 gives the proper response to the destruction the Lord brings to the earth at the end of the age. "Cease striving and know that I am God," or as it's sometimes translated, "Be still, and know that I am God!" (as in NLT). This verse is one of the most misinterpreted verses in the Bible.

Most often we hear this verse quoted as a call to contemplation and quiet reflection before God—of ceasing our frantic activity and busyness and resting before God. However, in the context of Psalm 46, where the final victory of the Messiah has just been described, this is not a call to contemplation or reflection but a redemptive call to surrender and know God personally before his judgment is unleashed.[9] It's a call to the nations to surrender. The Lord is calling humans to abandon their rebellion against him and to surrender to him.

God is saying, "You can never win your war against me, so quit while you can. Throw down your weapons and surrender."

In his book *God's Trombones*, James Weldon Johnson begins one poem about the Prodigal Son with these words: "Young man— / Young man— / Your arm's too short to box with God."[10] That's what the psalmist is saying here: "Give up the fight. Jesus is coming. His Kingdom is coming. Your arm is too short to box with God." The psalmist urges all people to surrender to him now.

According to Scripture, every knee will bow one day before Jesus (see Philippians 2:10). He will be exalted among the nations. Ultimate security will come for all who bow to the Lord. In the meantime, we find our security in bowing to him now and recognizing his presence with us in every circumstance of life.

Psalm 46:11 says, "The LORD of hosts is with us" (NASB). The words "with us" in the original Hebrew are one word, *immanu*, from which we get the word "Immanuel"—God with us. This is the name that Jesus would bear (see Matthew 1:23). The ultimate expression of God's presence with us is the coming of his Son Jesus Christ into the world to become one of us and to die in our place on the cross.

SAFE AND SOUND

As the last days march on and the signs of the times proliferate, we will all undoubtedly face more and more challenges to our personal and national security in an age of terror. We will all face daily challenges to our security in the arenas of health, finances, marriage, and family. But in all of this, remember—the answer to our problems, perils, and panic is the presence of God. We find our refuge and security in our great God. He's our fraidy hole as the storm clouds gather on the horizon.

There's a true story about a family from Canada that was consumed with fear about a coming war. They were terrified, so they decided to run away to the safest place on earth. After much research they found the perfect place, and in the spring of 1982 they relocated to this quiet little spot known as the Falkland Islands, an obscure piece of British real estate. The family relaxed and enjoyed five days of tranquility before the Argentineans invaded their backyard and began the famous Falklands War.

We sometimes wish we could run away from our fears and the things that make us feel insecure. But there's nowhere to run. Fear follows us. We can't outrun our fears. The only way to successfully overcome fear is to confront it and avail ourselves of God's resources. The Lord is our refuge and strength. He is our stronghold. When God is great, our fears are not. As our view of God expands, the fears of life diminish. As J. I. Packer reminds us, "The world dwarfs us all, but God dwarfs the world."[11] Allow Psalm 46 to expand your view of Christ and your fear of God.

Depend on him as your *Refuge*.

Draw upon him as your *River*.

Defer to him as your *Ruler*.

God is our *Refuge*; we need not fear.

God is also our *River*; we need not faint.

God is our *Ruler*; we need not fret.

A series of earthquakes rattled London in 1750, sending shock waves throughout the city. The first tremor struck on February 8. Early in the morning one month later, on March 8, Charles Wesley was preaching when a second earthquake hit. It was much stronger than the first one. As you can imagine, pandemonium ensued. Yet Wesley quoted Psalm 46 to the panicking parishioners. He later recounted how God had given him the words he needed to reassure the congregation.

Another earthquake rocked England's south coast just ten days later, prompting a man to predict a coming earthquake of even greater magnitude. The people believed his prophecy, fearing that the end of the world was near.

That prophecy never came to pass, but Charles Wesley published a collection of hymns that was written to calm the masses and came to be known as the "Earthquake Hymns." The collection includes a hymn based on Psalm 46.[12]

Our world is shaking today and feels like it's becoming less safe all the time. But even in tectonic times, remember: God is our Refuge, he is our River, and he is our Ruler.

THE BEST OF ALL, GOD IS WITH US

John Wesley, the great founder of Methodism (and brother of Charles) preached his final sermon on February 17, 1791, at age 87. The next day, feeling very ill and weak, he was put to bed in his home. During the days of his illness, he often repeated the words from one of his brother's hymns: "I the chief of sinners am, but Jesus died for me!" Wesley died on March 2, and as he lay dying, his friends gathered around him. He lovingly grasped their hands, saying, "Farewell, farewell." At the end, Wesley cried out, "The best of all is, God is with us." Lifting his arms, he raised his feeble voice one last time again, repeating the words, "The best of all is, God is with us."

If you know Jesus, you can say the same thing no matter what may come your way—"The best of all is, God is with us."

The presence of God is your ever-present, always-accessible fraidy hole as the end draws near.

CHAPTER 8

REMAIN UNDER THE INFLUENCE

All Christians are committed to be filled with the Spirit. Anything
short of a Spirit-filled life is less than God's plan for each believer.

BILLY GRAHAM

ON THE NIGHT BEFORE HE DIED, Jesus gave a long message to his closest followers sharing his heart with them about his coming departure and how they should live in his absence. The sermon known as the Upper Room Discourse is found in John 13–17. Jesus told his disciples many things, but he repeatedly mentioned the Holy Spirit, whom he would send to be with them in his physical absence (see John 14:15-17, 25; 15:26; 16:7-15).

Then, after his resurrection, just before he ascended to heaven, Jesus' final words to his followers were about the Spirit:

> "Do not leave Jerusalem until the Father sends you the gift he promised, as I told you before. John baptized with water, but in just a few days you will be baptized with the Holy Spirit. . . . But you will receive power when the Holy Spirit comes upon you. And you will be my witnesses, telling people about

me everywhere—in Jerusalem, throughout Judea, in Samaria, and to the ends of the earth." After saying this, he was taken up into a cloud while they were watching, and they could no longer see him.

ACTS 1:4-5, 8-9

Of all the things Jesus could have shared in his farewell address, he underscored the disciples' need for the presence and power of the Holy Spirit. If Jesus believed the Holy Spirit was important enough to mention over and over in his final instructions to his disciples, we need to take notice and learn about the Spirit's ministry in our lives in these end times. Nothing is more vital to your spiritual survival and success as you await Christ's coming than the Spirit.

Many believers today mouth the words about believing in the Spirit, but when it comes to their daily lives, he is out there somewhere on the periphery. Many today in the church are guilty of *loving* the Father, *adoring* the Son, and *ignoring* the Spirit.

In his classic book *Knowing God*, J. I. Packer calls the study of the Holy Spirit "the Cinderella of Christian doctrines" and adds, "Comparatively few seem to be interested in it."[1] Sadly, the Holy Spirit can be just a footnote in our theology—the minor key in our worship. Many Christians are settling for "two-thirds" of God. I once heard someone say, "The sin of the world is rejecting the Son; the sin of the church is neglecting the Spirit." We must make sure this isn't true of us. We need the Spirit's power to survive.

FOCUSING ON THE FILLING

There are many ministries of the Holy Spirit in the New Testament that we need to understand, but none is more central to the believer's daily life than the filling of the Spirit. Evangelist D. L. Moody once gathered a group of pastors together to discuss Christian holiness and productivity in daily living. At the end of their time together, Moody offered this summary: "I can tell you in five words how Christians can become more holy, useful, and fruitful—*be filled with the Spirit!*" Moody was right. These five words hold the key to our spiritual survival and service in these final days. There's no substitute.

In the troubled, temptation-filled times we all face, we're prone to believe that everything we do depends on us, that we simply have to try harder or be smarter, but we must not fall into the trap of thinking that we have the power to live the Christian life in our own strength. We can't live the Christian life without the filling of the Holy Spirit. We must have power beyond ourselves to flourish, especially in times like these. Simply stated, we can't survive spiritually without the work of the Spirit in our lives. Spiritual survival without the Spirit is a deadly oxymoron.

Spirit power is necessary for spiritual prosperity. Spirit saturation is necessary for spiritual survival. Spirit filling is necessary for spiritual flourishing.

But what does it mean to be filled with the Spirit?

The biblical entry point for understanding the Spirit-filled life is found in the book of Ephesians. Ephesians is a book that's rich in teaching about the Holy Spirit. Several key truths about the Spirit are highlighted:

> sealing of the Spirit (1:13; 4:30)
> accessing the Father through the Spirit (2:18)
> indwelling of the Spirit (2:19-22)
> unifying of the Spirit (4:1-3)
> grieving the Spirit (4:30)

Ephesians 5:16-21 is a key New Testament passage that tells us about the filling of the Spirit:

Make the most of every opportunity in these evil days. Don't act thoughtlessly, but understand what the Lord wants you to do. Don't be drunk with wine, because that will ruin your life. Instead, be filled with the Holy Spirit, singing psalms and hymns and spiritual songs among yourselves, and making music to the Lord in your hearts. And give thanks for everything to God the Father in the name of our Lord Jesus Christ. And further, submit to one another out of reverence for Christ.

This passage begins by telling us that we need to "make the most of every opportunity in these evil days." I don't have to tell you that the end times are evil days—not just bad days or tough days but downright evil days. We see it all around us. We've fallen so far that evil is now cool.

If we're to survive spiritually and "make the most of every opportunity" in evil days, the apostle Paul tells us that we must have a power and strength beyond ourselves. To put it bluntly, you will fail on your own. I will fail on my own. We are wholly inadequate on our own to meet the demands and challenges of life. We must stay under the influence of the Holy Spirit.

Since this is true, we need to look together at what it means to be filled with the Spirit, how we can be filled, and what it will look like if we're filled. Along with Bible study and prayer, nothing is more important to your spiritual survival than being Spirit-filled.

Learning about the Spirit-filled life was one of the major turning points in my own spiritual life. Knowing about the Spirit's power and influence available to me was life-changing. We need the Spirit's filling all the time, but in these evil days at the end of the age, our need is magnified even further.

THE MEANING

The best definition of being filled with the Spirit is being controlled or influenced by God the Holy Spirit—being under the influence of the Spirit. Where do we get this definition?

Vocabulary

The first key to understanding the filling of the Spirit comes from the vocabulary or terminology used. There are three Greek words used for the filling of the Spirit, and they all carry the idea of being controlled, influenced, or gripped by something. We observe the meaning of these words as they are used in other contexts, for example, the people in the synagogue being "filled with rage" when Jesus taught (Luke 4:28, NASB), sorrow having "filled" the hearts of the disciples when Jesus announced he was leaving them (John 16:6, NASB), Ananias allowing Satan to "fill [his] heart" in lying about the gift he brought to the apostles (Acts 5:3), and the false prophet Bar-Jesus being "full of every sort of deceit and fraud" (Acts 13:10). In the same way that these people were gripped or controlled by an emotion or outside force, believers are to be filled with the Holy Spirit.

Contrast

The second key is the contrast between drunkenness and the filling of the Spirit. Three times in the New Testament the filling of the Spirit is contrasted or at least mentioned in conjunction with getting drunk:

> He will be great in the eyes of the Lord. He must
> never touch wine or other alcoholic drinks. He will
> be filled with the Holy Spirit, even before his birth.
> LUKE 1:15

> Others in the crowd ridiculed them, saying, "They're just drunk, that's all!"
> Then Peter stepped forward with the eleven other apostles and shouted to the crowd, "Listen carefully, all of you, fellow Jews and residents of Jerusalem!

Make no mistake about this. These people are not
drunk, as some of you are assuming. Nine o'clock
in the morning is much too early for that. No, what
you see was predicted long ago by the prophet Joel:

'In the last days,' God says,
    'I will pour out my Spirit upon all people.
Your sons and daughters will prophesy.
    Your young men will see visions,
    and your old men will dream dreams.'"

ACTS 2:13-17

Don't be drunk with wine, because that will ruin
your life. Instead, be filled with the Holy Spirit.

EPHESIANS 5:18

Everyone knows that a person who is drunk is under the
control of alcohol. Drunkenness puts a person under the
influence of alcohol, and according to Ephesians 5:18, this
leads to a ruined life, or as the New American Standard Bible
has it, "dissipation." Notice in Ephesians 5:18 that being
drunk is contrasted with being filled with the Spirit. Just as
being drunk leads to being under the control of a foreign
influence, being filled with the Spirit leads to *his* control—
being under *his* influence.[2]

Both parts of this verse are equally true and operative—"don't
be drunk with wine" and "be filled with the Holy Spirit."
Both are commands (imperatives in Greek). Christians often

settle for half of this verse. We may not get drunk, but we also aren't filled with the Spirit. It's not enough not to be drunk with wine. Getting drunk is a sin of commission, while not being filled with the Spirit is a sin of omission.

I like the story of the children's Sunday school class where the teacher asked, "What is a sin of omission?" One little boy, after weighing the question, raised his hand and said, "Those are the sins we wanted to do but never got around to." Actually, sins of omission are *good* things we never got around to doing. Not being filled with the Spirit is a sin of omission.

Leighton Ford tells of a visit his brother-in-law, Billy Graham, made to a very large and influential church. His host told him of an unfortunate experience. One of the officers in that church had repeatedly gotten drunk, and so they had to discipline him and put him out of the church fellowship. Mr. Graham asked, "How long has it been since you put somebody out of the church for not being filled with the Holy Spirit?" His host looked startled. So Mr. Graham continued, "The Bible says, 'Don't get drunk with wine,' but the very same verse says, 'Be filled with the Spirit.'"

Billy Graham was making a valid point. The positive command to be filled with the Spirit is just as binding as the negative command not to be drunk with wine.

The Command

After the contrast between getting drunk with wine and being filled with the Spirit, we observe three important things about the command to be filled. First, the command is in the present tense. This indicates that it's an ongoing, repeated experience, not something that happens once for all. We could translate this as "Keep on being filled." Stanley Toussaint writes, "You can't go on last week's experience, last year's experience, or yesterday's experience. It is something that you must experience in the eternal *now*. Be filled with the Spirit constantly."[3]

There's an important distinction I need to point out between the *filling of the Spirit* and the *indwelling of the Spirit*. These are two distinct ministries of the Spirit. Believers in the New Testament are never commanded to be indwelled by the Spirit. Every believer in Christ has the Spirit from the moment of salvation (see Romans 8:9). The indwelling of the Spirit occurs once for all at the moment of salvation; the filling of the Spirit occurs again and again throughout our Christian life.

There's also a distinction between the *filling* of the Spirit and the *baptism* of the Holy Spirit. These two ministries of the Spirit are sometimes confused with one another. Every believer in Christ is baptized by Jesus into his body by the agency of the Spirit at the moment of conversion (see 1 Corinthians 12:13). The baptizing work of the Spirit is a universal, unrepeated work in the life of every believer.

The baptism and indwelling of the Spirit are part of the "standard" package that comes with salvation—they aren't optional equipment.[4] The fullness of the Spirit is received by every believer at the moment of conversion, but we must be filled (influenced and controlled) again and again. There is one indwelling and one baptism of the Spirit but many fillings.

As believers in Christ today, we are no longer waiting for the Holy Spirit; rather, *he* is waiting for *us*—waiting for us to surrender to him and yield our lives to him completely.

The filling of the Spirit must be repeated in our lives again and again.

There's an old story I heard years ago about a man who came forward to the altar every week at his church when the preacher asked who needed to dedicate their life to the Lord and get filled with the Spirit. After many weeks of the same routine, one man in the congregation turned to the man next to him and said, "Why does that man go down front every week to get filled with the Spirit? What's his problem?" The other man whispered back, "He leaks."

That's the problem for all of us. We leak. We must all be filled again and again.

Second, the command to be filled with the Spirit is *passive*. We could translate it "keep being continuously filled." It's something that's done to us. We allow it or yield to it. We allow the Spirit to take control of our lives. This makes all the difference.

I love the story about the medical doctor and evangelist Walter Lewis Wilson. Wilson was a believer who struggled with the futility and spiritual barrenness of his life. In 1913, a French missionary asked him, "Who is the Holy Spirit to you?" Wilson replied, "One of the Persons of the Godhead . . . Teacher, Guide, Third Person of the Trinity."

The missionary said, "You haven't answered my question." Wilson responded, "He is nothing to me. I have no contact with Him and could get along quite well without Him."

The next year, on January 14, 1914, Dr. Wilson heard James M. Gray preach a sermon on Romans 12:1: "I beseech you therefore, brethren, by the mercies of God, that ye present your bodies a living sacrifice, holy, acceptable unto God, which is your reasonable service" (KJV). Gray said, "Have you noticed that this verse does not tell us to whom we should give our bodies? It is not the Lord Jesus. He has His own body. It is not the Father. He remains on His throne. Another has come to earth without a body. God gives you the indescribable honor of presenting your bodies to the Holy Spirit, to be His dwelling place on earth."

The message hit home. Wilson went home, fell on the floor before the Lord, and prayed, "My Lord, I have treated You like a servant. When I wanted You, I called for You. Now I give You this body from my head to my feet. I give you my hands, my limbs, my eyes and lips, my brain. You may send this body to Africa, or lay it on a bed with cancer. It is your body from this moment on."

The following day two people came to his medical office selling advertising, and they both left believing in the Lord. From that point on, he was an effective, fruitful witness for the Lord—a Spirit-filled believer.[5] His life was changed. Surrendering to the Spirit made all the difference. Wilson was a dynamic personal evangelist and founded Central Bible Church in Kansas City, Flagstaff Mission to the Navajos, and the institute later to become Calvary Bible College. Wilson later wrote, "With regard to my own experience with the Holy Spirit, the transformation in my life on January 14, 1914 was much greater than the change that took place when I was saved."[6]

Surrendering to the Spirit makes all the difference.

The third key to the command is that it's *plural*, which means it's for every believer. The command to be filled with the Spirit is not just for pastors, elders, missionaries, mature believers, or some elite group. The Spirit-filled life is for every Christian. None of us are to get drunk. All of us are to be filled with the Spirit. Being Spirit-filled should be the normative experience of every Christian. Stanley Toussaint writes, "We *can* be filled with the Holy Spirit. All of us are to be filled with the Holy Spirit; it is a command. The filling of the Holy Spirit is the chassis—the drive train—of our Christian experience."[7]

In sum, being filled with the Spirit means we are to continuously allow our life to be controlled by the Spirit. The filling of the Spirit is not about me getting more of the Spirit but about the Spirit getting more of me. As I once heard someone say, the Spirit must not only be *resident* in our lives; he must be *president*.

There's another story I like about the famous preacher D. L. Moody and the filling of the Holy Spirit. Moody was scheduled to speak several places in England. In advance of his arrival, a meeting was held by several church leaders. A pastor protested, "Why do we need this 'Mr. Moody'? He's uneducated, inexperienced, etc. Who does he think he is anyway? Does he think he has a monopoly on the Holy Spirit?"

Another pastor responded, "No, but the Holy Spirit has a monopoly on Mr. Moody."[8] That's what every believer should desire for his or her life.

Now that raises a second key issue—how can you and I be Spirit-filled and remain under the influence?

THE MEANS

Not every believer in Jesus Christ is Spirit-filled. Every believer is Spirit-indwelled and Spirit-baptized but not necessarily Spirit-filled. There are certain spiritual conditions that must be met to experience the controlling of the Spirit. I've always found it interesting that there are no specific steps laid out in Ephesians 5:18 for being filled. No conditions are expressly given. There's no ritual or formula. The verb "be filled" is passive, so we know that this is something we allow to happen, not something we do ourselves. But how does it happen?

There's a sense in which we could say that "anybody who really loves the Lord Jesus and wants to please Him is *going to be filled* with the Holy Spirit."[9] We don't want to make the Spirit-filled life more complicated than necessary. A. W. Tozer says, "Throw your heart open to the Holy Spirit and invite Him to fill you. . . . Every man is as full of the Spirit as he wants to be. Make your heart a vacuum and the Spirit will rush in to fill it."[10]

Keeping this in mind, I do believe there are two main

clues or hints in other places in the New Testament about the means to being Spirit-filled. These two passages give us keys to how this filling takes place. The first is John 7:37-39, which calls on us to trust in the Lord:

> On the last day, the climax of the festival, Jesus stood and shouted to the crowds, "Anyone who is thirsty may come to me! Anyone who believes in me may come and drink! For the Scriptures declare, 'Rivers of living water will flow from his heart.'" (When he said "living water," he was speaking of the Spirit, who would be given to everyone believing in him. But the Spirit had not yet been given, because Jesus had not yet entered into his glory.)

The first attitude that puts us under the Spirit's influence is trust in the Lord ("everyone believing in him"). It's coming to the Lord and saying, "I need you. I trust in you. I can't live today in my own strength. I put myself under your control."

The second passage is Colossians 3:16-17, which calls us to open our lives to God's Word and obey it. Note the striking parallels between Ephesians 5:18-21 and Colossians 3:16, which reads, "Let the message about Christ, in all its richness, fill your lives. Teach and counsel each other with all the wisdom he gives. Sing psalms and hymns and spiritual songs to God with thankful hearts."

Ephesians and Colossians are often considered tandem epistles by the apostle Paul, written about the same time during his first Roman imprisonment and delivered by the same courier. There's a clear correlation between what Paul says in Ephesians 5:18-21 about being filled with the Spirit and what he says in Colossians 3:16-17 about letting Christ's word dwell within you. The results of each are the same, so they appear to be parallel. This shouldn't surprise us, since the Spirit is the Author of the Word. The two are always in sync.

This means that allowing the Word to richly dwell within, to be at home in our lives, is a key means for the Spirit to take over. We must give our minds to the truth of God's Word, our hearts to its teaching, and our wills to its commands. To be open to the Word and under its influence is to place ourselves under the control of the Spirit. I once heard a preacher say, "When the Word dwells within us, the Spirit swells within us."

The means of being filled is to trust in the Lord and open our hearts and lives to his Word. Any heart that is open toward God and in submission to the Scriptures will be filled with the Spirit. When we do these things, the Spirit takes over and goes to work.

So what happens when a believer is filled with the Spirit? What does it look like? How do you know if you're Spirit-filled?

THE MANIFESTATIONS

I don't know if you've noticed, but anytime the New Testament speaks of someone being filled with the Spirit, it's always followed by the word "and." There's always an "and" to the work of the Spirit. There are always results of being filled with the Spirit. What are those results we should be looking for? What will a life look like when the Spirit takes over?

First, notice what's not in Ephesians 5:19-21. Not flashy, spectacular, sensational experiences—speaking in tongues, being slain in the Spirit, being translated into some ecstatic state, or miraculous signs and wonders. The focus is rather on three main manifestations, which are all in the present tense, indicating that these results are continual and ongoing in the life of the Spirit-filled believer.

Music (Gladness)

The first result of the Spirit's control is a glad heart full of joy manifested in music.

Ephesians 5:18-19 says, "Be filled with the Holy Spirit, singing psalms and hymns and spiritual songs among yourselves, and making music to the Lord in your hearts." We're to sing from our hearts, not just move our lips, and "to the Lord"—our songs are directed to the one who delivered us from wrath and gives us the power to live a life that pleases him. God wants to hear you sing to him with all your heart. God wants to hear you sing praises to him.

A Spirit-filled Christian is a joyful, singing Christian who loves to praise the Lord for his greatness, grace, mercy, goodness, and majesty. Do you love to sing? Do you go around every day with a song in your heart? A Spirit-filled Christian is a singing Christian and lives a life filled with joy and music.

It's a dead giveaway. The same is true of churches. Dead churches and dead Christians don't sing; "they just kind of stand there and mumble."[11]

Thankfulness (Gratefulness)

The second manifestation or result of being filled with the Spirit is a thankful heart. This means a Spirit-filled believer is not bitter, grumbling, complaining, negative, sour, or grumpy but thankful and grateful. There are four key aspects to our thankfulness to God.

When are we to give thanks? "Always" (NASB).

What are we to give thanks for? "Everything."

Whom are we to give thanks to? "God the Father."

How are we to give thanks? "In the name of our Lord Jesus Christ."

We understand giving thanks for the good things, and we can even understand giving thanks "*in* everything" (1 Thessalonians 5:18, NASB). But "*for* everything" is a different matter. How do we give thanks "always . . . for all things" (NASB)? Does this include even sin? John Stott clarifies the meaning:

God abominates evil, and we cannot praise or thank him for what he abominates.

So then the "everything" for which we are to give thanks to God must be qualified by its context, namely *in the name of our Lord Jesus Christ to God the Father*. Our thanksgiving is to be for everything which is consistent with the loving Fatherhood of God and the self-revelation he has given us in Jesus Christ.[12]

Spirit-filled believers are thankful.

Submission (Graciousness)

A third manifestation of the Spirit's control is submission. This refers to repenting of self-centeredness and putting others ahead of ourselves. Submissive people are concerned about others, are concerned about what others think, and think of others, not just themselves.[13] Spirit-filled submission is humble and gracious.

So, *what is the Spirit-filled life?* A life under the influence and control of the Spirit.

How can we be filled? By trusting in the Lord and obeying God's Word.

What are the results of being filled? Gladness, gratefulness, and graciousness.

Today, as evil abounds, there are all kinds of opportunities around us. We need to be filled with the Spirit to meet the demands of life. We can't do it in our own strength. What follows Ephesians 5:18-21 is a discussion of marriage, family, and work (5:22–6:9). We all know how broken and hurting the family is today. The Spirit-filled life spills over into every area of our relationships. We have to be Spirit-filled to have marriages and families that please the Lord and witness to the world around us.

HOLD ON

A. J. Gordon, one of the founders of Gordon-Conwell Theological Seminary, told of seeing a house across a field when he was out walking, with a man vigorously using a hand pump next to the house. The man was pumping rapidly without ever slowing down or resting. Amazed at this sight, Gordon walked toward it until he saw it was not a man after all, but a painted wooden figure. Wire held the hand to the pump, and the water pouring out came from an artesian well. Rather than the man pumping the water, the water was pumping the man.

When you see a person whose work for the Lord is effective and produces results—someone who is filled with gladness, gratefulness, and graciousness—that is a person who is filled with the Holy Spirit. When we keep our hands on the pump, the Spirit will fill us and use us. [14]

When this happens, you won't just survive spiritually; you will thrive, and others will be blessed by and through you.

Your spouse needs a Spirit-filled husband or wife.

Your family needs a Spirit-filled mother or father.

Your church needs a Spirit-filled member.

Your friends need a Spirit-filled companion.

Your neighbors need a Spirit-filled neighbor.

Your community needs a Spirit-filled citizen.

The days are evil. Depravity and darkness are spreading. Redeem the time. Take full advantage of every opportunity. But don't try to go it alone.

Whatever else you do in life, make sure you remain under the influence of the Holy Spirit.

Your spiritual survival depends on it.

CHAPTER 9

TUNE IN TO HEAVEN'S FREQUENCY

The world hopes for the best, but Jesus Christ offers the best hope.

JOHN WESLEY WHITE

WHEN THE WISCONSIN BADGERS were playing the Michigan State Spartans in October 1982, Badger Stadium was packed with expectant fans. It began to seem, however, that Michigan State might have the better team.

Despite the uncertainty of the game, and at seemingly inappropriate times, the Wisconsin fans erupted in cheers and applause. How could devoted fans be so excited when there wasn't any cause for celebration on the field?

On the same day as the Wisconsin Badgers game, the Milwaukee Brewers were playing the St. Louis Cardinals in game four of the 1982 World Series. Many of the Badgers fans that day were watching their team struggle on the field but listening to the Brewers win. While what they could see on the field at times looked grim, they were cheering a victory they could not see.[1]

This story resonates with me because it reminds me of our present situation on earth as God's people. Let's face it—here on earth things don't seem to be looking too good for God's team. As believers, it can sometimes feel like our team is losing . . . and losing badly. We see it around the world on many fronts. The church is suffering persecution in many places, where believers are severely mistreated and even martyred for their faith. Closer to home, believers are frequently the object of mocking and maligning. In courts, workplaces, schools, and the halls of government, people have become increasingly unwelcoming and even antagonistic toward those who follow Jesus. Watching the "game" as it unfolds in front of us can be difficult at times and can even diminish our hope and drive us to despair.

But like those beleaguered Badgers fans, while we're watching the game in front of us, at the same time, we can tune in to another "game" and cheer on a victory that's invisible to us now but no less real—a total victory in heaven that's coming soon to planet Earth.[2]

This world needs hope. You and I need hope. And our only hope as the score gets more and more lopsided down here is to stay tuned in to heaven's frequency, listening and looking every day for the final victory that's coming through Jesus Christ.

IS THERE ANY HOPE?

On December 17, 1927, a US submarine off the coast of Massachusetts was attempting to surface when it was struck by a US Coast Guard destroyer and sank immediately. The crew scrambled to secure themselves behind watertight doors. The entire crew was entombed in a prison house of death. Every effort was made to rescue the crew, but nothing worked. Near the end of the ordeal, a diver put his ear to the side of the vessel and heard a faint tapping from inside. Recognizing it as Morse code, he heard the same question formed slowly over and over—"Is . . . there . . . any . . . hope?"[3]

That's the key question people everywhere are asking today: "Is there any hope?" There's a growing hopelessness out there today—even among some believers.

I like the story about the wife who said to her husband, "Should we watch the six o'clock news and get indigestion or wait for the eleven o'clock news and have insomnia?" That's about how bad it's gotten. Key questions on the minds of many people are "Where is everything headed?" "What's the world coming to?" and "Is there any hope?"

One of the most quoted Old Testament passages in the New Testament answers this question as clearly and succinctly as possible. Let's look now at Psalm 2.

LIFE'S TWO GREAT QUESTIONS

The first two psalms are the driveway into the Psalms. Their positioning in the book of Psalms is deliberate. They answer the two great questions of life. Psalm 1 answers the question, *Where am I going?* This is the most urgent individual matter. The psalm, in more traditional translations, opens with the word "blessed" and ends with the word "perish." This psalm sets forth two paths for humanity—the way of the righteous (those who receive the Lord and are blessed) and the way of the wicked (those who reject the Lord and perish). Every person falls into one of these two groups. Every person needs to make sure he or she belongs to the community of the righteous through faith.

Psalm 2 answers the second great question: *Where is the world going? Where is history headed?*

That's why these psalms are Psalms 1 and 2. We meet the two great issues of life at the front door of the Psalms. I need to know where I'm going, and I need to know where history is going.[4] I need to see the whole show. You and I need to have a biblical worldview in these last days to buoy our lives and fill us with hope. We need to know the end game.

Psalm 2 is God's decisive declaration of the outcome of world events. There's no greater comfort in the chaotic, uncertain times in which we live than to know where it's all headed. Psalm 2 is all about hope for planet Earth. More specifically, it's about hope for planet Earth in Jesus Christ. It tells us that the world has been promised to the Messiah. His triumph is certain. Here is Psalm 2 in its entirety:

Why are the nations so angry?
   Why do they waste their time with futile plans?
The kings of the earth prepare for battle;
   the rulers plot together
against the LORD

and against his anointed one.
"Let us break their chains," they cry,
    "and free ourselves from slavery to God."

But the one who rules in heaven laughs.
    The Lord scoffs at them.
Then in anger he rebukes them,
    terrifying them with his fierce fury.
For the Lord declares, "I have placed my chosen king on
      the throne
    in Jerusalem, on my holy mountain."

The king proclaims the LORD's decree:
"The LORD said to me, 'You are my son.
    Today I have become your Father.
Only ask, and I will give you the nations as your
      inheritance,
    the whole earth as your possession.
You will break them with an iron rod
    and smash them like clay pots.'"

Now then, you kings, act wisely!
    Be warned, you rulers of the earth!
Serve the LORD with reverent fear,
    and rejoice with trembling.
Submit to God's royal son, or he will become angry,
    and you will be destroyed in the midst of all your
      activities—

for his anger flares up in an instant.
But what joy for all who take refuge
in him!

Before we probe deeper into Psalm 2, let's get a brief understanding of its background. Psalm 2 is one of the most frequently quoted psalms in the New Testament. According to Acts 4:25, David is the author of this psalm. It's a messianic psalm. We know this because it's quoted in the New Testament as referring to Jesus. It's been called the Drama of the Ages. Psalm 2 outlines the agelong rebellion of mankind against God and his Son and how it all ends in God's victory. At its core, it's a psalm of hope.

Psalm 2 is divided into four parts or stanzas, each with a different speaker, but I want to look at it under two headings derived from our image of the Badgers' football game: "The Chaos We See" and "The Conquest We Can't See."

Watching the game in front of us here on earth can push us to despair. Of course, we have to live here on this earth and watch the game on the field. But if we have no farther horizon, no outside perspective beyond this world, we will lose hope quickly. Our spiritual survival will be in jeopardy. We can't survive long without hope. Tuning in to heaven's frequency is our only hope. Listening and learning about the invisible victory going on far away is our ultimate encouragement. But before we consider what's happening on heaven's frequency, let's begin by surveying the scene that's unfolding before our eyes.

THE CHAOS WE SEE

The first stanza of Psalm 2 unveils a shocking, agelong, global insurrection and conspiracy against God. In this stanza the speaker or voice is that of the nations or lost humanity.

The first word of Psalm 2 is "Why?" or we could translate it "How could they?" The psalmist can hardly believe what he sees and hears. He sees "the rulers plot together against the LORD and against his anointed one," which is a reference to the Messiah.

Here we witness the nations rising up in cosmic treason against God and his Messiah in rebellion against God's sovereignty. The Bible says that lost humanity is against God and Jesus. I know that may sound strong, but that's what the Bible says. In fact, that's what Jesus says too (see John 15:18). The rage of humanity against God may not show up with the same fury at all times in all places, but its strong undercurrent is always present. The world hates God, detests his Messiah, and despises Messiah's people.

Lost humanity may love the Jesus they've created but not the Jesus who is God in human flesh and the only way to God. The world is against the real Jesus.

What could possibly possess people to have such rage against the true God and his Son?

The defiant voice of sinners, banded together in their rebellion, speak with one collective voice in Psalm 2:3: "Let us break their chains and free ourselves from slavery to God."

What lost humanity wants more than anything is freedom from God. This is the heart of sin, a rejection of God's rule in favor of our own. The lost don't want God to reign over them. People want what they want with no restraints.

The world wants sexual freedom. The sexual revolution began in the 1960s and was followed by changing attitudes toward homosexual behavior that continues today. The result is pervasive immorality, the pollution of pornography, and the peril of widespread gender confusion. Carl F. H. Henry once described the modern generation as "intellectually uncapped, morally unzippered and volitionally uncurbed."[5] That's what we see today.

The world also wants intellectual freedom. Against all reason, they hold doggedly to the notion that all the beauty, order, and constancy of creation came about by the collision of time and chance. And because the created order is the result of random chance, marriage can be redefined by judicial fiat.

Lost humanity wants spiritual freedom. They want to decide whether there is a God, and if there is a God, they want to decide who he is and how they come to him. I love the words of the Scottish theologian P. T. Forsyth: "The first duty of every soul is to find not its freedom but its Master."[6] But lost humanity wants it the other way around. Yet sadly, the search for freedom results in deeper enslavement. It results in chaos. Because of unrestrained freedom, our world is a mess and reeling out of control. We live in a world gone wild. It's tragic to see the resulting chaos and confusion in homes, schools, lives, and marriages.

When people lose God, they lose themselves. That's what

we see in Romans 1:18-32—the tragic consequences of defying the Lord and his Christ. Paul says of lost humanity, "Claiming to be wise, they instead became utter fools. . . . Since they thought it foolish to acknowledge God, he abandoned them to their foolish thinking and let them do things that should never be done. Their lives became full of every kind of wickedness" (verses 22, 28-29).

As Frederick Buechner says, "The power of sin is centrifugal. When at work in a human life, it tends to push everything out toward the periphery. Bits and pieces go flying off until only the core is left. Eventually bits and pieces of the core itself go flying off until in the end nothing at all is left."[7]

This ongoing, agelong rebellion of lost humanity against God and his Son began in the Garden of Eden, continues today, and will stretch all the way to the second coming of Christ.

According to Acts 4:23-31, the premier historical example of this rebellion occurred in the crucifixion of Jesus. The apostles quote Psalm 2 and fill in the blanks with Herod and Pilate.

Comparing the rebellion of modern man with what happened at the tower of Babel, Os Guinness observes, "In their vaunting pride, advanced modern humanists are competing with their ancient rivals in rebellion. They are straining every nerve and brain cell to make a name for their projects and themselves. But they too are driven by an insatiable need to succeed, for only success after success can allow them to avert their eyes from the strains and stresses on humanity and on the earth behind them."[8]

We have front-row seats to this game as human rebellion

is on full display. God has placed us here to live and witness for him. We must represent heaven here on earth. We're not just spectators; we're in the game. We're ambassadors for Christ to this lost world (see 2 Corinthians 5:20). We're to do all we can while we can. Individuals must be rescued from the uprising against God.

Nevertheless, Scripture tells us that the rebellion of this world won't improve. It's going to get worse as the end nears. But praise God! There's a frequency we can listen to every day that inspires us with an invisible victory that is going on now in heaven and is coming to earth someday, maybe very soon.

THE CONQUEST WE CAN'T SEE

Tuning in to heaven's frequency—the invisible victory—we hear about final victory on planet Earth from three sovereign voices: the voice of the Father, the voice of the Son, and the voice of the Spirit. What we have here is powerful inter-Trinitarian communication.

The Voice of the Father—Mockery

Heaven's response to earth's upheaval begins with the voice of God the Father. The response of the Father to humanity's rebellion is laughter. Yes, God laughs: "The one who rules in heaven laughs. The Lord scoffs at them" (Psalm 2:4). This is the only time recorded in the Bible when God laughs. This is not the laughter of humor or hilarity but divine derision, mockery, and contempt.

God openly mocks humanity's puny rebellion. God is

not fazed in the slightest. He's unimpressed. As the prophet Isaiah reminds us, "All the nations of the world are but a drop in the bucket. They are nothing more than dust on the scales. He picks up the whole earth as though it were a grain of sand" (Isaiah 40:15).

But if God is sovereign over this world, we might look around at the mess we see and wonder, *Why doesn't God do something? Why doesn't God fix it all right now?* As I heard someone say, "I know God is in control, but sometimes I wish he would make it more obvious." We all probably share that sentiment sometimes.

Psalm 2 assures us that someday God *will* make his control obvious. He will do this by installing his Son on a throne on earth: "I have placed my chosen king on the throne in Jerusalem, on my holy mountain" (Psalm 2:6).

Most scholars believe Psalm 2 is a "Royal Psalm," that it relates to the coronation of the kings of Judah. Many see it as going beyond Solomon and his successors, ultimately pointing to the Messiah. While some reference to human kings is possible, I prefer to view this psalm as about Jesus only. Several things said here cannot be said of any king other than Jesus. For instance, only to Jesus will the whole earth be given as his possession. Christ is presently enthroned in heaven, but Psalm 2 looks ultimately to the return of Christ to earth and his glorious enthronement on David's throne and his thousand-year rule of peace and prosperity over the earth (see Revelation 20:1-6).

Notice in Psalm 2:6 that the placing of Jesus on David's

throne to rule the world is stated in the past tense ("I *have placed* my chosen king on the throne"). It's as good as done. Nothing can stand in the Son's way.

The Voice of the Son—Victory

That brings us to the third stanza, where the speaker shifts from the Father to the Son of God—the Messiah. All that the Father has planned and purposed in eternity will be performed by the Son in history. The decree of Yahweh controls history. The Son says,

> The LORD said to me, "You are my son.
>   Today I have become your Father.
> Only ask, and I will give you the nations as your
>   inheritance,
>   the whole earth as your possession.
> You will break them with an iron rod
>   and smash them like clay pots."
>
> PSALM 2:7-9

When Jesus comes back to this earth, he will come as King of kings and Lord of lords to inherit a global kingdom, putting a sudden, sweeping end to the agelong rebellion of man (see Daniel 7:14, 27; Revelation 20:1-6).[9] Jesus will destroy rebellious humanity. He will do it with ease, effortlessly, like someone smashing fragile clay pots with an iron rod.

Josiah Wedgwood was an English potter, the founder of the Wedgwood company, and he is known as the one responsible for the industrialization of pottery. He would often walk through his factory in England and smash inferior pieces of pottery with his walking stick, saying, "This will not do for Josiah Wedgwood."

There's a day coming when Jesus will smash to pieces everything that is contrary to his will. He will, in essence, say, "This won't do for the Son of God." He will take the planet back and restore paradise.

Jesus is saying to us, "Don't tolerate now what I won't tolerate then. If it won't do for Christ in the future, put it out of your life now. Don't be ruled by the world that will someday be ruled by Christ."

The Voice of the Spirit–Opportunity

The final stanza in this psalm records the message of the Holy Spirit speaking through the psalmist. The Spirit's invitation goes out to all who will receive the Son. Instead of resisting God, sinners must turn from sin and self and serve the Lord with fear. The choice is clear. Those who fail to bow in submission to the Son have a rendezvous with judgment. As Old Testament scholar Derek Kidner says, "There is no *refuge* from him: only *in him*."[10] One day, "those who worshipped him on earth will confess him gladly. Those who didn't will confess him regretfully."[11]

C. S. Lewis poignantly describes the coming of Christ's victory to earth:

> God will invade. . . . When that happens, it is the
> end of the world. When the author walks on to the

stage the play is over. . . . For this time it will be God without disguise; something so overwhelming that it will strike either irresistible love or irresistible horror into every creature. It will be too late then to choose your side. . . . That will not be the time for choosing: it will be the time when we discover which side we really have chosen, whether we realised it before or not. Now, today, this moment, is our chance to choose the right side. God is holding back to give us that chance. It will not last for ever. We must take it or leave it.[12]

Jesus came the first time in mercy, to save. The second time he will come in wrath, to judge. The end-times events predicted in the Bible are all lining up. The stage is being set. We see the buildup all around us. The signs of the times point to the soon coming of the Lord Jesus Christ.

He may be coming soon. Our decision to submit to him is urgent.

Jesus is earth's only hope. He is *your* only hope. He is *my* only hope.

Let me close this chapter with four simple applications or meditations to give us hope in a world gone wild and to ensure our spiritual survival.

1. YOU CAN'T UNDERSTAND HISTORY APART FROM JESUS CHRIST

Jesus alone holds the key to the meaning of history. The world has been promised to the Messiah. All of history is wrapped up in him. History culminates in his second coming to earth to rule and reign over the earth (see Revelation 19:11–20:6). George Eldon Ladd states, "Here is a simple but profound biblical truth which cannot be overemphasized: apart from the person and redeeming work of Jesus Christ, history is an enigma. . . . Christ, and Christ alone, has the key to the meaning of human history."[13] James Hamilton adds,

> We need Jesus.
>
> We need Jesus not only for our own personal salvation. We need Jesus so there is hope for the world. By his death and resurrection Jesus has taken control of history. Jesus has seized destiny—not just his destiny—all destiny. Jesus is the one who ensures that the universe will have meaning. Jesus is the one who will judge the wicked and vindicate those who have trusted in him. Jesus is the one who will right the wrongs and heal the hurts and wipe away the tears.
>
> We need Jesus. Without Jesus there is no hope.[14]

I like the story of a father who was intently watching the final minutes of a close football game on television, when his little boy came running in, asking him to play. The father sent him away with promises that he would play soon, but the son kept coming back at intervals and asking if it was time yet.

Searching for anything that would allow him to watch the game in peace, the father saw a picture of the world on a newspaper in front of him and tore it into pieces, like a jigsaw puzzle. The father gave the pieces to his son and said, "When you've put the picture back together, then it will be time to play."

Thinking this task would take his son a while, the father settled in to watch the remainder of the game. But no sooner had he settled in than his son returned with the picture of the world reassembled. "I did it, Daddy," he said. "Is it time now?"

The father couldn't believe that his son had finished the puzzle so quickly, but there it was: the world was taped back together. "How did you do this so quickly?" the father asked.

"It was easy," the boy said. "I saw there was a picture of Jesus on the other side, and when I put that picture together, the world came together too."[15]

When Jesus is put together in his rightful place, the world comes together. Jesus is the only one who puts the world together. He is the Alpha and Omega.

2. HISTORY IS HEADED TO THE FEET OF JESUS

Have you ever wondered what the world is coming to? If Psalm 2 tells us anything, it tells us that the world is coming to Jesus. In spite of how things look on earth, Psalm 2 assures us that Jesus rules. His Kingdom is coming to earth, and all must bow to him. This is the ultimate worldview.

The sculptor Bertel Thorvaldsen created a marble statue of Christ that was placed in the National (Lutheran) Cathedral in Copenhagen, Denmark. The figure's arms are extended, welcoming all who will come. Yet the statue has an unusual feature. To look directly into the face of the statue, it's necessary to kneel. It's impossible to get a clear view from any other position.

A famous story recounted from English literature concerns the essayist Charles Lamb and a group of literary men who began to surmise what they would do if the noble and gifted men of the past were to enter into the room. They began to call out the names of various greats and what they would do if that person appeared in their midst. Lamb said, "If Shakespeare were to enter, we would rise to our feet in admiration for his accomplishments. But if Jesus Christ were to enter, we would fall down at His feet and worship Him in adoration."[16]

Bertel Thorvaldsen and Charles Lamb were dead right. The only proper response to the person and presence of Jesus Christ—who is eternal God—is to fall on our knees or on our faces in wonder and adoration. We don't rise in *admiration* to shake his hand; we fall in *adoration* to kiss his feet.

All of history is ultimately headed to the feet of Jesus Christ. If all history is headed there, that's where we should live our lives now in humble worship as we await his coming.

The words of P. T. Forsyth capture the essence of our humble worship: "The world thus finds its consummation not in finding itself, but in finding its Master; not in coming to its true self but in meeting its true Lord and Saviour; not in overcoming but in being overcome."[17]

We overcome, not by overcoming, but by being overcome in awestruck worship of our Savior.

3. JESUS IS IN TOTAL CONTROL OF THE PRESENT AND THE FUTURE

Although it looks today like evil is unchecked and humanity's rebellion is triumphing, the invisible victory in heaven today is real and will be manifest soon on earth.

There's a great story about Ray Stedman when he was in England years ago preaching in some London churches. On one occasion he spoke in a Methodist chapel, and the congregation was singing "Our God Reigns," which was a new song at that time. However, when Stedman looked at the song sheet the congregation was using, he noticed that the typist had made an error. Instead of "Our God Reigns," the song was titled "Our God Resigns."

That's a funny story, but many Christians live that way today, as if God has resigned. All they can see is the game on the field in front of them. But God has not resigned. Rather, as the song says, our God *reigns*! Stedman writes, "This is what we must declare. We must show it on our faces, and let it be heard in our voices."[18] Jesus is coming someday as King.

Every day should find us "Singing in the Reign" as we anticipate and celebrate the coming of Jesus to take his inheritance.

On April 15, 1865, President Abraham Lincoln died at 7:22 a.m. At that moment, the doctor whispered, "He is gone." As others in the room knelt by Lincoln's bedside, a minister prayed that God would receive his servant Abraham

Lincoln into heaven. The room then fell silent until Secretary of War Edwin Stanton poignantly declared, "Now he belongs to the ages."[19]

Some humans, like Abraham Lincoln, are so great in their impact that they belong to the ages, but only of Jesus can we truthfully say that the ages belong to *him*. Jesus controls the destiny of the ages. He will triumph over the world.

4. WE CAN REST TODAY IN OUR KNOWLEDGE OF WHAT'S COMING AND WHO'S COMING IN THE FUTURE

Kent Crockett tells this story: "A mother asked her son why he always read the end of the book first. The boy replied, 'Mom, it's better that way. No matter how much trouble the hero gets into, I don't have to worry, because I know how it's going to end.'"[20]

I like that. God has announced to us how the story will end. Jesus wins, Satan loses, and all who trust in Jesus will live happily ever after.

In the meantime, as we await the final victory, we live in a turbulent world. The chaos and rebellion in the world are real. There's no way to mitigate the current condition of planet Earth. But we must not let the "game" we see dampen our spirits and plant seeds of hopelessness in our hearts. Don't give in to despair and cynicism. As Corrie ten Boom reminds us, "Look at yourself, you'll get depressed, look at the world, you'll get distressed, look at Jesus, you'll find rest."

As the score down here gets more lopsided, tune in every day to heaven's frequency and check the score up there. It's all under control. The victory is sure, and all who submit to Jesus will share his triumph.

Today's *invisible* victory will soon become his *invincible* victory.

Don't give up. Don't give in. Don't give out.

The best is yet to come!

CHAPTER 10

WAKE UP

Let us be alert to the season in which we are living. It is the
season of the Blessed Hope. . . . It is imperative that we stay fully
alert to the times in which we live. . . . All signs today point to this
being the season of the Blessed Hope. . . . All around us, we have the
evidence of Jesus' soon return. Each day our focus should be on
the Coming One. Our focus on the Blessed Hope is the most
important discipline of our Christian life.

A. W. TOZER

POLLING REVEALS THAT MOST AMERICAN EVANGELICALS have
a sense that the end times are upon us. The Religion News
Service reported that according to a 2013 poll, "41% of all
U.S. adults, 54% of Protestants and 77% of Evangelicals
believe the world is now living in the biblical end times."[1]
   Polls have also found that

> 58 percent of Americans think that another world war
   is "definite or probabl[e]."
> 41 percent "believe Jesus Christ will return" by the
   year 2050.
> 59 percent "believe the prophecies in the Book of
   Revelation will come to pass."[2]

Further, "research conducted by the Brookings Institute's Center for Middle East Policy on Americans' attitudes toward the Middle East and Israel found that 79 percent of Evangelicals say they believe 'that the unfolding violence across the Middle East is a sign that the end times are nearer.'"[3] These statistics reveal that people everywhere, and especially evangelicals, believe history is winding down—that the world is getting near closing time.

As a result, some Christians are overly focused on Christ's return. It's all they think about. They're preoccupied with prophecy. This leads to all kinds of unhealthy speculation such as recklessly setting dates for Christ's return, spending countless hours "prepping" for the apocalypse, trying to figure out the identity of the Antichrist and the meaning of 666, and seeing every flood, earthquake, eclipse, or hurricane as a significant sign of the times.

The majority of believers, however, seem to lean toward the other extreme with at best a tepid interest in Jesus' coming. These sluggish, slumbering saints are hitting the snooze button rather than waking up and watching for Jesus' coming.

In his teaching about the end of days, Jesus presents a balance between these two extremes we see today—between the alarmists and the apathetic. Jesus calls on his followers to be awake and alert.

LAST-DAYS LIVING

Jesus talked often about the future. He may have talked about the future more than any person who ever lived. In the New

Testament, "Jesus refers to His second coming 21 times, and over 50 times we are told to be ready for His return."[4] Jesus wasn't preoccupied with the end times in an unbalanced way. He always talked about the future to change the way people live in the present.

The call to readiness dominated the teaching of Jesus, especially in the final days of his life on earth. Time and again, he emphasized that his followers must keep watching and stay alert. In his great prophetic sermon in Mark 13, delivered just days before he died on the cross, Jesus gives the basic blueprint or outline of the events that will immediately precede his coming. This sermon, often called the Olivet Discourse since it was given by Jesus on the Mount of Olives just to the east of Jerusalem, is also recorded in Matthew 24–25 and Luke 21.

In this sermon, Jesus provides a litany of signs that will portend his return to earth. Jesus clearly teaches about signs of the times. He says that the generation that sees these signs will witness his second coming to earth (see Mark 13:30). However, this sermon is much more than a list of signs of the times. Jesus highlights how his followers are to live in light of his coming.

He says, "You, too, must *keep watch*! For you don't know what day your Lord is coming. Understand this: If a homeowner knew exactly when a burglar was coming, he would *keep watch* and not permit his house to be broken into. You also must *be ready* all the time, for the Son of Man will come when least expected" (Matthew 24:42-44, emphasis added).

The parable of the ten bridesmaids should reverberate in our hearts with a call to readiness:

> The Kingdom of Heaven will be like ten bridesmaids who took their lamps and went to meet the bridegroom. Five of them were foolish, and five were wise. The five who were foolish didn't take enough olive oil for their lamps, but the other five were wise enough to take along extra oil. When the bridegroom was delayed, they all became drowsy and fell asleep.
>
> At midnight they were roused by the shout, "Look, the bridegroom is coming! Come out and meet him!"
>
> All the bridesmaids got up and prepared their lamps. Then the five foolish ones asked the others, "Please give us some of your oil because our lamps are going out."
>
> But the others replied, "We don't have enough for all of us. Go to a shop and buy some for yourselves."
>
> But while they were gone to buy oil, the bridegroom came. Then those who were ready went in with him to the marriage feast, and the door was locked. Later, when the other five bridesmaids returned, they stood outside, calling, "Lord! Lord! Open the door for us!"
>
> But he called back, "Believe me, I don't know you!"

So you, too, must keep watch! For you do not know the day or hour of my return.

MATTHEW 25:1-13

Notice all the bridesmaids fall asleep, but five are ready and five are not. Jesus' point is simple: only those who are ready and prepared will enter his Kingdom.

In Mark's account of Jesus' sermon, he closes with a clear call to spiritual alertness. As you read these words, notice the repeated use of "watch" and "stay alert."

Now learn a lesson from the fig tree. When its branches bud and its leaves begin to sprout, you know that summer is near. In the same way, when you see all these things taking place, you can know that his return is very near, right at the door. I tell you the truth, this generation will not pass from the scene before all these things take place. Heaven and earth will disappear, but my words will never disappear.

However, no one knows the day or hour when these things will happen, not even the angels in heaven or the Son himself. Only the Father knows. And since you don't know when that time will come, *be on guard! Stay alert!*

The coming of the Son of Man can be illustrated by the story of a man going on a long trip. When he left home, he gave each of his slaves instructions

about the work they were to do, and he told the
gatekeeper to *watch* for his return. You, too, must
keep watch! For you don't know when the master
of the household will return—in the evening, at
midnight, before dawn, or at daybreak. *Don't let him
find you sleeping* when he arrives without warning. I
say to you what I say to everyone: *Watch* for him!

MARK 13:28-37, EMPHASIS ADDED

Jesus refers to the four watches of the night according to
Roman reckoning: evening, midnight, before dawn ("cock-
crow"), and daybreak. He emphasizes that he can come at
any time.[5] Vigilance is required.

The apostles followed Jesus' lead and issued the call to
readiness to their generation. Their words are a much-needed
wake-up call:

This is all the more urgent, for you know how late it
is; time is running out. Wake up, for our salvation is
nearer now than when we first believed. The night is
almost gone; the day of salvation will soon be here.

ROMANS 13:11-12

They speak of how you are looking forward to the
coming of God's Son from heaven—Jesus, whom
God raised from the dead. He is the one who has
rescued us from the terrors of the coming judgment.

I THESSALONIANS 1:10

Be on your guard, not asleep like the others. Stay alert and be clearheaded.

I THESSALONIANS 5:6

Look, I will come as unexpectedly as a thief! Blessed are all who are watching for me, who keep their clothing ready so they will not have to walk around naked and ashamed.

REVELATION 16:15

The reference in that final verse to having clothes stripped off and walking around naked may be an allusion to what happened to guards in that day who fell asleep. Their punishment was having their clothes stripped off and burned and being sent home naked and in disgrace.[6]

The message is clear: those waiting for Christ to come must fight spiritual drowsiness.

I like the story of the college professor who would walk into the lecture hall each morning and place a tennis ball on the corner of his podium. The tennis ball didn't seem to have any purpose—at the end of the lecture, the professor would put it back in his jacket pocket and leave. The students wondered why he did this but were never quite sure—until a student fell asleep in class. The professor walked over to the podium and, without any change in his intonation or notes, picked up the tennis ball and fired it at the sleeping student, scoring a direct hit on his head.

At class the following day, the professor placed a baseball

on the podium. The entire class was wide awake from then on.[7]

The words of Jesus should serve as a tennis ball to the head for those of us who are drowsy and dozing in these last days. With all that's going on in our world today, we have every reason to be awake and alert. In these last days, Jesus should have our rapt attention.

AWAKE AND ALERT

I hope you're convinced that Jesus is coming, that he could come at any time, and that you need to be watchful and alert. John MacArthur tells a great story that underscores this truth:

> Jesus is telling you, "I'm coming, I'm coming." I remember a preacher was preaching on the second coming. And he was one of those guys who believed that you shouldn't have any notes, you ought to preach strictly off your head. And he forgot his point. All he could remember was, "Behold, I come quickly; behold, I come quickly." And it should have jogged his mind, so he said it about five times and nothing happened. The final time he thought, "If I hit the pulpit real hard and say, 'Behold, I come quickly,' maybe something will jar loose and I'll remember." Instead he knocked the pulpit over and fell in the lap of a lady in the first row. And he apologized. She said, "Why are you apologizing? You

warned me eight times you were coming." She got the point.[8]

I hope *we* get the point. Jesus places high value on his followers being awake and alert. The Rapture is possible any day, impossible no day. In light of the imminence of Christ's coming, the key issue that should grab our hearts is being alert and awake. That's what Jesus repeated over and over.

So, what does it look like for a believer today to be watchful and alert?

What It Doesn't Mean

One thing we know "watching" doesn't mean is setting dates for Christ's coming.

Jesus clearly says, "No one knows the day or hour when these things will happen, not even the angels in heaven or the Son himself. Only the Father knows. And since you don't know when that time will come, be on guard! Stay alert!" (Mark 13:32-33). The two parables Jesus employs, the fig tree and the gatekeeper, further demonstrate that no one can know the exact time of the Master's return (see Mark 13:28-29, 34).

Speculating about the precise moment of Jesus' return is not part of faithful preparation. For any person to claim to know what even Jesus did not know during his sojourn on earth is the height of arrogance and folly. The litany of signs in Mark 13 demonstrates that followers of Jesus can know the general season of Christ's return—otherwise they wouldn't be signs. Nevertheless, Jesus says no one on earth can know the time of his coming. The issue for faithful disciples is not calendars and clocks but commitment. Never listen to anyone who claims to know the time of Jesus' coming. Whenever someone sets a date for Christ's coming, you can be sure that's not the date.

Second, waiting for Christ is not passive, like waiting at a bus stop for the bus to show up. Waiting and watching for Jesus is active. Mark 13 contains nineteen specific imperatives or commands from Jesus. This should let us know that being awake and alert for his coming requires action.

Moreover, the parable Jesus gives in Mark 13:34 depicts a man going away on a journey and assigning various tasks for his servants while he's away. This parable instructs us that watching for Jesus is not just sitting around passively waiting; rather, it involves keeping the house ready for his arrival. The beds must be made, the floors must be swept, and the garden must be tended. Watching is more than just waiting, looking up into the heavens every day.

There's a story I've told before about a bunch of sailors returning from a long voyage at sea. As the boat approached shore the men were all looking for their wives and girlfriends on the shore, eager to see them. As the men searched the crowd of women lined up, the air of excitement and expectancy grew. One sailor, however, was left all alone as all the other men found their wives and girlfriends. His wife wasn't there.

Worried, he rushed home and found a light on. He

was relieved to see his wife when he went inside. She said, "Honey, I'm so glad to see you. I've been waiting for you!" His response displayed his disappointment. "The other men's wives and girlfriends were *watching* for them!"

Likewise, Jesus doesn't call us to be passive waiters but to be active, engaged watchers.

What It Does Mean

Jesus emphasizes at least three main actions that fill in for us what it looks like to be alert and awake in the last days. The first is *protection*. We must stand strong in the truth and guard our lives from spiritual deception. The sermon in Mark 13 begins with these words from Jesus: "See to it that no one misleads you" (NASB). He later adds the warnings "Be on your guard" and "Take heed" (verses 9, 23, NASB). The repeated warnings are clear that we must be on guard against false teaching that will proliferate as Christ's coming draws near.

Referring to the parable of the gatekeeper in Mark 13:34, Ray Stedman says:

> Now, what is he to watch for? Is he to watch for the master's return? That is the way this is usually interpreted. But that is not it, for he is to start watching as soon as the master leaves. They know he will not be back right away. What then is he to watch for? He is to watch lest somebody deceive them and gain entrance into the house, and wreck

THE END TIMES SURVIVAL GUIDE

and ruin and rob all they have. . . . Don't let
anything derail you from being what God wants you
to be in this day and age. This is the way you watch.
We are not to be looking up into the sky all the time,
waiting for his coming. That will happen when he is
ready. We are to watch that we are not deceived.[9]

Alertness involves protection. And what is the best defense
against the false teaching and deception that will proliferate
in the end times? Knowing the truth of God contained in the
Bible. Staying awake and alert means we must read, study,
and apply the Bible for ourselves and also regularly listen to
gospel-centered, biblical preaching at a local church. Charles
Swindoll says, "In this age of darkness, we can't afford to
doze off spiritually. We need to stay awake. We need to keep
our eyes open and our Bibles open, avoiding dangerous
deception."[10]

Second, spiritual alertness includes *preparation*. We can't
be ready and alert if we're unprepared. Mark's Gospel gives
us an important clue about what it means to be prepared
for Christ's coming. Mark uses a literary device known
as an inclusio to make his point. An inclusio consists of
similar material placed before and after a specific text that
serves to bracket, bookend, or frame the text, emphasiz-
ing what is most important in the section in between the
bookends.

Mark 13 is strategically bracketed by two accounts of
"unnamed women who are the epitomes of faithfulness,

194

demonstrating incredible loyalty and devotion to God."[11] The preceding bookend is the poor widow in Mark 12:42-44, who gives everything she has to the Lord. She's the gold-medal giver in the Bible. The following bookend is an unnamed woman who anoints Jesus' feet with expensive perfume (see Mark 14:1-9). Her sacrifice is "profuse, pure, and precious."[12] By bookending chapter 13 with these two stories, Mark gives clear examples of the lavish sacrifice and devotion that characterize preparedness. Being prepared for the Lord's return includes liberally sacrificing our time, money, talents, and energy to serve the Lord's interests and to help others.

How prepared is your life for the coming of Christ? Are you awake, alert, active, and attentive, using what you've been given in the Lord's service? Or are you dull and drowsy?

Steven Cole relates this personal story about always being prepared:

> I once worked at the swanky Drake Hotel in
> Chicago. Years before I was there, in July of 1959,
> Queen Elizabeth was scheduled to visit Chicago.
> Elaborate preparations were made for her visit. The
> waterfront was readied for docking her ship. Litter
> baskets were painted and a red carpet was ready to
> be rolled out for her to walk on. Many hotels were
> alerted to be ready. But when they contacted the
> Drake, the manager said, "We are making no plans
> for the Queen. Our rooms are always ready for
> royalty."[13]

Make sure your life is always ready for royalty. Live each day alert and prepared by laboring and living sacrificially for our coming King as we await his arrival.

I like a story I've heard about preacher Warren Wiersbe. As the story goes, when he was a young preacher, his account of end-times prophecy was meticulously crafted and left little margin for guesswork. After one service where he laid out his account, a member of the congregation approached him and said, "I used to have the Lord's return planned out to the last detail, but years ago I moved from the planning committee to the welcoming committee."[14]

Wiersbe explains, "This does not mean that we should stop studying prophecy, or that every opposing viewpoint is correct, which is an impossibility. But it does mean that, whatever views we hold, they ought to make a difference in our lives."[15] The focus of end-times prophecy is not to build a calendar but to change our lives in preparation for our Lord's coming.

The third aspect of our alertness for last-days living is *proclamation*. In Mark 13:10, Jesus says, "The Good News must first be preached to all nations." Jesus is saying that before he comes again, all the world must hear the gospel. This doesn't have to be fulfilled before Jesus comes for his bride at the Rapture, but it must happen before Jesus can return to earth at the end of the future time of tribulation.

Part of our marching orders for last-days living is faithfully proclaiming the gospel (see Matthew 28:18-20). How can we legitimately claim to be awake and alert and at the same time be oblivious to the perishing world around us? Watching and witnessing go together. We can't get so caught up in our own ambitions and pursuits that we turn a blind eye and a deaf ear to those around us who don't know Jesus. Neither can we get so caught up in the details of the end times that we lose sight of the spiritual needs that surround us. As my friend Randall Price says,

> What good is it to be able to understand the seven heads described in Revelation 13:1 if we don't use our own head? Or what profit is it to discern the ten toes of Daniel 2 . . . if we don't move our own two feet? And what value is it to know about the great mouth that speaks lies (Daniel 7:8; Revelation 13:5), unless we open our own mouth and speak the truth? In every generation where prophecy has been properly proclaimed, the results have been a harvest of souls to the glory of God.[16]

We need to ask the Lord every day to give us opportunities to be witnesses for him. He wants to use us more than we want to be used.

The famed evangelist D. L. Moody had many positive practices in his life, but one is especially worth attempting to emulate. Moody committed to share the gospel with someone every day. He didn't want a day to go by without telling someone about Jesus. R. A. Torrey, a close friend of Moody, tells this story:

Mr. Moody got home and had gone to bed before
it occurred to him that he had not spoken to a soul
that day about accepting Christ. "Well," he said to
himself, "it is no good getting up now; there will be
nobody on the street at this hour of the night." But
he got up, dressed and went to the front door. It was
pouring rain. "Oh," he said, "there will be no one out
in this pouring rain." Just then he heard the patter
of a man's feet as he came down the street, holding
an umbrella over his head. Then Mr. Moody darted
out and rushed up to the man and said: "May I share
the shelter of your umbrella?" "Certainly," the man
replied. Then Mr. Moody said: "Have you any shelter
in the time of storm?" and preached Jesus to him.[17]

May God help us to have at least something of Moody's
heart for the lost as this age draws to a close. Alertness includes
being on the lookout every day for those around us who
haven't found spiritual refuge in Jesus from the coming storm.
Let's not fall asleep on the job.

I CAN SEE CLEARLY NOW

I had to get glasses in sixth grade to correct my bad near-
sightedness. A couple of years later I was able to get contact
lenses and lose the obnoxious glasses (this was back before
glasses were fashionable). Hard contact lenses have been an
integral part of my life since then.

Everything was fine until my early forties, when my

close-up vision started to get fuzzy. Reading almost anything became a chore. I refused to surrender to the problem because I thought my only option was to get reading glasses or bifocals. But the frustration finally drove me to get help. To my surprise, my optometrist told me about another option called monovision. With monovision the dominant eye is corrected to 20/20 for distance while the other eye is corrected for near vision. It took about a week for my brain to adjust to the new situation, but since then it has been fantastic. I can see 20/20 far away and clearly up close—with no glasses.

Watching for the coming of Jesus is like spiritual monovision. We're to always be watching the horizon for his coming with one eye, anticipating his return, yet at the same time seeing plainly what's up close that needs our attention as we live our daily lives. Jesus knows we need both lenses to live a balanced life.

Spiritually, if all we have is distance vision we miss the up-close obligations and opportunities of everyday life, but if all we have is near vision, we lose perspective and life gets fuzzy and out of focus. We need both. Jesus wants us watching and working—awake and active.

ULTIMATE SURVIVOR

The bestselling book *Unbroken* captured the world's attention as it chronicled the survival of Louis Zamperini for forty-seven days stranded in a rubber raft after his B-24 malfunctioned and was ditched in the Pacific during World War II. One man didn't survive the ordeal, but Zamperini and the pilot were finally retrieved by Japanese sailors and endured more than two harrowing years in a Japanese POW camp, where he was the object of vicious brutality by a guard nicknamed "The Bird."

After the war ended in 1945, Zamperini returned home but found no peace. Rage, shame, violent flashbacks, and constant nightmares consumed him. Zamperini had survived physically but was dead spiritually.

With his drinking out of control, both Zamperini and his new marriage were falling apart. In October 1949, Zamperini was desperate, so he went to hear Billy Graham preach in Los Angeles and received Christ as his Savior. He found peace for the first time in his life. In his book *Devil at My Heels*, he tells about the beginning of his spiritual survival:

> [I] asked Jesus to come into my life. I waited. And then, true to His promise, He came into my heart and my life. The moment was more than remarkable; it was the most *realistic* experience I'd ever had. I'm not sure what I expected; perhaps my life or my sins or a great white light would flash before my eyes; perhaps I'd feel a shock like being hit by a bolt of lightning. Instead, I felt no tremendous sensation, just a weightlessness and an enveloping calm that let me know that Christ had come into my heart.[18]

What a description—"a weightlessness," "an enveloping calm." That's what Jesus gives to all who turn to him in simple faith and trust. The Bible describes it like this: "We praise God for the glorious grace he has poured out on us who belong to his dear Son. He is so rich in kindness and grace that he purchased our freedom with the blood of his Son and forgave our sins" (Ephesians 1:6-7).

As you finish this book, make sure you're alive and awake spiritually. Make sure you've found the ultimate secret to spiritual survival. Do what Louis Zamperini did: trust Jesus. Receive him and his forgiveness. Let him lift your burden. Experience the wonderful weightlessness of grace.

Remember, Jesus is coming for those who have come to him.

Come to him now.

Be an ultimate survivor.

NOTES

INTRODUCTION: ULTIMATE SURVIVOR

1. Ed Hindson, *Final Signs: Amazing Prophecies of the End Times* (Eugene, OR: Harvest House, 1996), 191.
2. Erwin W. Lutzer, *Where Do We Go from Here? Hope and Direction for Our Present Crisis* (Chicago: Moody, 2013), 39.
3. Sean Sullivan, "5 Moments That Show Why Margaret Thatcher Mattered in American Politics," *The Washington Post,* April 8, 2013, https://www .washingtonpost.com/news/the-fix/wp/2013/04/08/5-moments-that-show -why-margaret-thatcher-mattered-in-american-politics/.
4. Howard LaFranchi, "Margaret Thatcher: 'This Is No Time to Go Wobbly' and Other Memorable Quotes," *Christian Science Monitor,* April 8, 2013, https://www.csmonitor.com/USA/Foreign-Policy/2013/0408/Margaret -Thatcher-This-is-no-time-to-go-wobbly-and-other-memorable-quotes.
5. Os Guinness, *Impossible People: Christian Courage and the Struggle for the Soul of Civilization* (Downers Grove, IL: IVP Books, 2016), 195.
6. Megan G. Oprea, "Why America Is Obsessed with Survivalism," *Federalist,* March 28, 2016, http://thefederalist.com/2016/03/28/why-america-is -obsessed-with-survivalism/.
7. Lutzer, *Where Do We Go from Here?,* 44.
8. I believe the Rapture will occur before the Tribulation, so I don't think believers will be on earth for the final period of Great Tribulation before the second coming of Jesus to earth. This is commonly called the pre-Tribulational view of the timing of the Rapture. If you want to know more about the various views of the timing of the Rapture and why I believe the pre-Tribulational view is most consistent with Scripture, see my book *The End: A Complete Overview of Bible Prophecy and the End of Days* (Carol Stream, IL: Tyndale, 2012), 121–88.

CHAPTER 1: USE THE 46 DEFENSE

1. Doug Farrar, "How Ryan's 46 Defense Ruled Football," *Sports on Earth*, June 28, 2016, http://www.sportsonearth.com/article/186694084/buddy -ryan-46-defense-bears-eagles-nfl.

2. Robinson Meyer, "The Most Popular Passages in Books, according to Kindle Data," *Atlantic*, November 2, 2014, https://www.theatlantic.com /technology/archive/2014/11/the-passages-that-readers-love/381373/.

3. Robert J. Morgan, *Worry Less, Live More: God's Prescription for a Better Life* (Nashville: W Publishing Group, 2017), xv.

4. Jim Folk and Marilyn Folk, "Anxiety Disorder Statistics," AnxietyCentre .com, April 25, 2017, http://www.anxietycentre.com/anxiety-statistics -information.shtml.

5. Don Joseph Goewey, "85 Percent of What We Worry about Never Happens," *HuffPost* (blog), August 25, 2015, https://www.huffingtonpost .com/don-joseph-goewey-/85-of-what-we-worry-about_b_8028368.html.

6. Morgan, *Worry Less, Live More*, 55.

7. Horace Greeley, *The Autobiography of Horace Greeley: Or, Recollections of a Busy Life* (New York: E. B. Treat, 1872), 405.

8. Morgan, *Worry Less, Live More*, 53.

9. "From Spurgeon's 'Faith's Check Book,'" Gospel Web, September 24, 2014, http://www.gospelweb.net/SpurgeonDevotions/Spurgeon0330.htm.

10. Morgan, *Worry Less, Live More*, 120.

11. "Spurgeon's 'Faith's Check Book.'"

12. Steven J. Lawson, *Philippians for You* (Purcellville, VA: The Good Book Company, 2017), 197.

13. James Montgomery Boice, *The Sermon on the Mount: Matthew 5–7* (Grand Rapids, MI: Baker Books, 2006), 223.

CHAPTER 2: RUN FOR YOUR LIFE

1. Philip De Courcy, "Run for Your Life," Know the Truth, June 30, 2015, https://www.ktt.org/resources/truth-matters/run-your-life.

2. Ibid.

3. William Barclay, *The Letter to the Hebrews*, rev. ed. (Louisville, KY: Westminster John Knox Press, 1976), 171.

4. Joe Stowell, "The Great Race," Strength for the Journey, http://getmore strength.org/daily/the-great-race/.

5. Ibid.

6. R. Kent Hughes, *Hebrews: An Anchor for the Soul*, vol. 2 (Wheaton, IL: Crossway Books, 1993), 160.

7. J. C. Ryle, *Heading for Heaven* (Reprint, Carlisle, PA: EP Books, 2009), 33–34.

8. Os Guinness, *Impossible People: Christian Courage and the Struggle for the Soul of Civilization* (Downers Grove, IL: IVP Books, 2016), 55.

9. Max Lucado, *Max on Life: Answers and Insights to Your Most Important Questions* (Nashville: Thomas Nelson, 2010), 207.

10. Ibid.

11. Eric Alexander, "Keep On," Ligonier Ministries, September 1, 2012, http://www.ligonier.org/learn/articles/keep-on/.

CHAPTER 3: MAKE A GOOD CONNECTION

1. John S. Dickerson, *The Great Evangelical Recession: 6 Factors That Will Crash the American Church . . . and How to Prepare* (Grand Rapids, MI: Baker Books, 2013), 98.

2. Ibid., 99.

3. Ibid.

4. Ibid.

5. Thom S. Rainer, "The Number One Reason for the Decline in Church Attendance and Five Ways to Address It," *Christian Post*, August 23, 2013, http://www.christianpost.com/news/the-number-one-reason-for-the-decline-in-church-attendance-and-five-ways-to-address-it-102882/.

6. Donald S. Whitney, *Spiritual Disciplines within the Church: Participating Fully in the Body of Christ* (Chicago: Moody, 1996), 16.

7. Alex Almario, "The Myth of Steve Jobs and the Truth about Us," Philstar Global, September 18, 2015, http://www.philstar.com /supreme/2015/09/19/1501293/myth-steve-jobs-and-truth-about-us.

8. Kevin DeYoung, "Stop the Revolution. Join the Plodders," Ligonier Ministries, September 9, 2016, http://www.ligonier.org/blog/stop-the -revolution-join-the-plodders/.

9. Ibid.

10. "No Excuse Sunday," BibleBelievers.com, https://www.biblebelievers.com /NoExcuseSunday.html.

11. Erwin W. Lutzer, *Where Do We Go from Here? Hope and Direction for Our Present Crisis* (Chicago: Moody, 2013), 39.

12. Anne Lamott, "Finding Our Way Home," *Our Daily Bread* (Grand Rapids, MI: RBC Ministries), quoted at "Philippians Illustrations 2," Precept Austin, February 21, 2015, http://www.preceptaustin.org /philippians_illustrations_2.

13. Doug McIntosh, *Life's Greatest Journey: How to Be Heavenly Minded and of Earthly Good* (Chicago: Moody, 2000), 30.

14. David Jeremiah, *Living with Confidence in a Chaotic World: What on Earth Should We Do Now?* (Nashville: Thomas Nelson, 2009), 93.

15. "The Lonely Ember," StoriesforPreaching.com, https://storiesforpreaching .com/category/sermonillustrations/church/.

16. This list is adapted from Mike Hubbard, "The 'One Anothers' of the New Testament," Genesis Church, September 6, 2009, https://blog.genesis eureka.com/2009/09/06/the-one-anothers-of-the-new-testament/.

17. Moniek, "On Pain of Death, Do Not Touch Queen Sunandha!" History of Royal Women, June 5, 2015, https://www.historyofroyalwomen.com /sunandha-kumaritana/on-pain-of-death-do-not-touch-queen-sunandha/.

CHAPTER 4: PUT ON YOUR ARMOR

1. Peter Berger, quoted in Os Guinness, *Impossible People: Christian Courage and the Struggle for the Soul of Civilization* (Downers Grove, IL: InterVarsity Press, 2016), 77–78.

2. Lesslie Newbigin, *Lesslie Newbigin: Missionary Theologian: A Reader*, comp. Paul Weston (Grand Rapids, MI: William B. Eerdmans, 2006), 47.

3. Quoted by Ray Pritchard, *Stealth Attack: Protecting Yourself against Satan's Plan to Destroy Your Life* (Chicago: Moody, 2007), 18.

4. Ray C. Stedman, *Spiritual Warfare: How to Stand Firm in the Faith* (Grand Rapids, MI: Discovery House, 1999), 20–21.

5. S. Lewis Johnson, "The Christian's Conflict" (sermon, Believer's Chapel, Dallas, TX, 2006), https://s3-us-west-2.amazonaws.com/sljinstitute -production/new_testament/Ephesians/18_SLJ_Ephesians.pdf.

6. D. Martyn Lloyd-Jones, *The Christian Soldier: An Exposition of Ephesians 6:10-20* (Grand Rapids, MI: Baker Books, 1977), 179.

7. Stedman, *Spiritual Warfare*, 133.

8. Ibid., 134, 136, 137.

9. James Montgomery Boice, *Ephesians: An Expositional Commentary* (Grand Rapids, MI: Baker Books, 1997), 253.

10. David Jeremiah, *Spiritual Warfare* (San Diego, CA: Turning Point, 2002), 80.

11. A. W. Tozer, *Born after Midnight* (Chicago: Moody, 2015), 52.

CHAPTER 5: KEEP PUSHING

1. Charles R. Swindoll, *Finding God When the World's on Fire: Strength & Faith for Dangerous Times* (Franklin, TN: Worthy Inspired, 2016), 8–9.

2. S. D. Gordon, *Quiet Talks on Prayer: When Praying People Engage a Giving God, Amazing Things Are Bound to Happen*, rev. ed. (Uhrichsville, OH: Barbour, 2013), 17–18.

3. Quoted at Danny E. Olinger, "Prayer and the Ministry," Orthodox Presbyterian Church, reprinted from *New Horizons* (February 2006), https://www.opc.org/nh.html?article_id=62.

4. Quoted in J. I. Packer & Carolyn Nystrom, *Praying: Finding Our Way through Duty to Delight* (Downers Grove, IL: IVP Books, 2006), 213.

5. E. M. Bounds, *E. M. Bounds on Prayer* (Peabody, MA: Hendrickson, 2006), 198.

6. Thomas Watson, *The Lord's Prayer*.

7. Haddon W. Robinson, *What Jesus Said about Successful Living: Principles from the Sermon on the Mount for Today* (Grand Rapids, MI: Discovery House, 1991), 200.

8. Martin Luther, "Small Catechism" quoted at Ray Pritchard, "Daily Bread Living" (sermon, Keep Believing Ministries, October 8, 2009), http://www.keepbelieving.com/sermon/daily-bread-living/.

9. Hudson Taylor, quoted at John Stott, "Four Things John Stott Learned from Hudson Taylor," OMF, November 30, 2016, https://omf.org/uk/2016/11/30/four-things-john-stott-learned-from-hudson-taylor/.

10. Philip Graham Ryken, *The Prayer of Our Lord*, rev. ed. (Wheaton, IL: Crossway Books, 2002), 76.

11. George Herbert, quoted in Ryken, *The Prayer of Our Lord*, 76.

12. P. T. Forsyth, *The Soul of Prayer* (Vancouver, BC: Regent College, 2002), 16.

13. Ben Patterson, *Deepening Your Conversation with God: Learning to Love to Pray* (Minneapolis: Bethany House, 2001), 28.

14. Robinson, *What Jesus Said about Successful Living*, 192.

15. Warren W. Wiersbe, *Prayer 101: Experiencing the Heart of God* (Colorado Springs: David C Cook, 2016), 84.

CHAPTER 6: DO THE BEST THINGS IN THE WORST TIMES

1. Joseph M. Stowell, *Shepherding the Church: Effective Spiritual Leadership in a Changing Culture* (Chicago: Moody Press, 1997), 15.

2. D. Edmond Hiebert, *1 Peter* (Chicago: Moody Press, 1992), 268–69.

3. Wayne Grudem, *1 Peter*, Tyndale New Testament Commentaries, ed. Leon Morris (1988; repr., Grand Rapids, MI: Eerdmans, 1997), 172–73.

4. Daniel L. Segraves, *First Peter: Standing Fast in the Grace of God* (Hazelwood, MO: World Aflame Press, 1999), 239.

5. Stuart Briscoe, *1 Peter: Holy Living in a Hostile World*, Understanding the Book series, rev. ed. (Wheaton, IL: Harold Shaw Publishers, 1993), 167.

6. Warren W. Wiersbe, *The Bible Exposition Commentary*, New Testament, vol. 2 (Wheaton, IL: Victor Books, 1989), 422.

7. Charles R. Swindoll, *Insights on James, 1 & 2 Peter*, Swindoll's New Testament Insights (Grand Rapids, MI: Zondervan, 2010), 218.

8. Edmund Clowney, *The Message of 1 Peter*, The Bible Speaks Today, ed. John R. W. Stott (Downers Grove, IL: IVP, 1988), 179.

9. Erwin W. Lutzer, *Where Do We Go from Here? Hope and Direction for Our Present Crisis* (Chicago: Moody, 2013), 38.

10. Max Lucado, "Open Your Door, Open Your Heart," UpWords, October 8–14, *Christianity.com*, https://www.christianity.com/devotionals /upwords-max-lucado/open-your-door-open-your-heart-upwords-week-of -october-8-14-11639250.html.

11. "Hospitality," *Preaching.com*, https://www.preaching.com/sermon -illustrations/hospitality/.

12. Denis Lyle, "Failures in Our Relationship to the Holy Spirit," SermonIndex .net, http://www.sermonindex.net/modules/articles/index.php?view=article &aid=22498.

13. Ray C. Stedman, *From Guilt to Glory*, vol. 2 (Palo Alto, CA: Discovery, 1978), 118–19.

14. "Humility," Chinese Christian Bible Study Data Website, http://ccbiblestudy .net/Topics/89Character/89GE20.htm.

CHAPTER 7: FIND YOUR FRAIDY HOLE

1. Steven Lawson, "Luther and the Psalms: His Solace and Strength," October 15, 2012, Ligionier Ministries, https://www.ligonier.org /blog/luther-and-psalms-his-solace-and-strength/.

2. David Jeremiah, *Slaying the Giants in Your Life* (Nashville: Thomas Nelson, 2001), 3.

3. Charles R. Swindoll, *Living the Psalms: Encouragement for the Daily Grind* (Brentwood, TN: Worthy Publishing, 2012), 134.

4. Warren W. Wiersbe, *The Bumps Are What You Climb On* (Grand Rapids, MI: Baker Books, 2002), 141.

5. Bob Abramson, "The Power of a Spider Web," Mentoring Ministry, March 26, 2013, https://www.mentoringministry.com/2013/03/the-power-of-a -spider-web/.

6. Erwin W. Lutzer, *Where Do We Go from Here? Hope and Direction for Our Present Crisis* (Chicago: Moody, 2013), 25.

7. Robert J. Morgan, *The Strength You Need: The Twelve Great Strength Passages of the Bible* (Nashville: W Publishing Group, 2016), 63–64.

8. Swindoll, *Living the Psalms*, 138–39.

9. Steven J. Lawson, *Psalms 1–75*, Holman Old Testament Commentary, gen. ed. Max Anders (Nashville: Holman Reference, 2003), 246.

10. James Weldon Johnson, *God's Trombones* (New York: Penguin Books, 2008), 21.

11. J. I. Packer, *Knowing God* (Downers Grove, IL: InterVarsity Press, 1973), 8.

12. Morgan, *The Strength You Need*, 67.

CHAPTER 8: REMAIN UNDER THE INFLUENCE

1. J. I. Packer, *Knowing God* (Downers Grove, IL: InterVarsity Press, 1973), 68.
2. Stanley D. Toussaint, "Living in the Power of the Holy Spirit," *Veritas* (July 2004), Dallas Theological Seminary, http://www.dts.edu/download /publications/veritas/veritas-2004-july.pdf. Much of the information in this chapter is adapted from this brief article and time in classes with Dr. Toussaint at Dallas Theological Seminary when I was a student.
3. Toussaint, "Living in the Power of the Holy Spirit," 6.
4. David Jeremiah, *God in You: Releasing the Power of the Holy Spirit in Your Life* (Sisters, OR: Multnomah, 1998), 89.
5. Robert J. Morgan, *On This Day: 365 Amazing and Inspiring Stories about Saints, Martyrs & Heroes* (Nashville: Thomas Nelson, 1997), January 14.
6. Ibid.
7. Toussaint, "Living in the Power of the Holy Spirit," 6.
8. "D. L. Moody," Bible.org, https://bible.org/node/10435.
9. Toussaint, "Living in the Power of the Holy Spirit," 3.
10. A. W. Tozer, *Man: The Dwelling Place of God* (Camp Hill, PA: WingSpread, 2008), 39.
11. Toussaint, "Living in the Power of the Holy Spirit," 5.
12. John R. W. Stott, *The Message of Ephesians*, The Bible Speaks Today, ed. John R. W. Stott (Leicester, England: Inter-Varsity Press, 1979), 207.
13. Toussaint, "Living in the Power of the Holy Spirit," 6.
14. Max Anders, *What You Need to Know about the Holy Spirit in 12 Lessons* (Nashville: Thomas Nelson, 1995), 140.

CHAPTER 9: TUNE IN TO HEAVEN'S FREQUENCY

1. "Cheering the Invisible Victory," *Preaching Today*, http://www.preaching today.com/illustrations/1998/july/4466.html.
2. We can see this victory in some ways today. Despite the persecution of Christians, Christianity is actually growing across the non-Western world.
3. Ben Patterson, *Serving God: The Grand Essentials of Work & Worship*, rev. ed. (Downers Grove, IL: InterVarsity Press, 1994), 39.
4. Dale Ralph Davis, *The Way of the Righteous in the Muck of Life: Psalms 1–12* (Scotland: Christian Focus Publications, 2010), 27–28.
5. Quoted at Steve Kumar, "The Battle for Truth," *Think Why?*, November 20, 2008, https://thinkwhy.wordpress.com/2008/11/20/the-battle-for-truth/.
6. Richard Lischer, ed., *The Company of Preachers: Wisdom on Preaching, Augustine to the Present* (Grand Rapids, MI: Eerdmans, 2002), 100.

7. Frederick Buechner, *Beyond Words: Daily Readings in the ABC's of Faith* (New York: HarperCollins, 2004), 368–69.

8. Os Guinness, *Impossible People: Christian Courage and the Struggle for the Soul of Civilization* (Downers Grove, IL: IVP Books, 2016), 139.

9. The kingdom spoken of in Psalm 2 is not a present, spiritual kingdom. It's the future, literal, earthly, Davidic kingdom promised in 2 Samuel 7:12-16. Two points in Psalm 2 support this view. First, "Jerusalem" is mentioned as the place where Messiah's throne will be established. There's no reason in Psalm 2 to take this in any way other than literally. Second, Messiah's kingdom will be established not by *salvation* but by *subjugation*. This supports a future, literal kingdom and argues against any notion of a present spiritual kingdom that is being slowly expanded by the preaching of the gospel.

10. Derek Kidner, *Psalms 1–72*, Kidner Classic Commentaries (Downers Grove, IL: InterVarsity Press, 2008), 70.

11. Max Lucado, *Because of Bethlehem* (Nashville: Thomas Nelson, 2016), 115.

12. C. S. Lewis, *Mere Christianity* (New York: HarperCollins, 2001), 65.

13. George Eldon Ladd, *A Commentary on the Revelation of John* (Grand Rapids, MI: Eerdmans, 1972), 82.

14. James M. Hamilton Jr., *Revelation: The Spirit Speaks to the Churches*, Preaching the Word, ed. R. Kent Hughes (Wheaton, IL: Crossway, 2012), 151.

15. "The World Is a Puzzle," StoriesforPreaching.com, https://storiesfor preaching.com/the-world-is-a-puzzle/.

16. Sinclair B. Ferguson, *Child in the Manger: The True Meaning of Christmas* (Carlisle, PA: Banner of Truth Trust, 2016), 177.

17. P. T. Forsyth, *The Justification of God: Lectures for War-Time on a Christian Theodicy* (Eugene, OR: Wipf and Stock, 1999), 227.

18. Ray Stedman, "Our God Reigns," Daily Devotions, News and Information, February 24, 2016, https://808bo.com/2016/02/24/ray-stedman-our-god -reigns/.

19. Now He Belongs to the Ages," April 15, 2008, *Lincoln Studies: Abraham Lincoln and the American Civil War*, http://lincolnstudies.blogspot.com /2008/04/now-he-belongs-to-ages.html/.

20. Kent Crockett, *Making Today Count for Eternity* (Sisters, OR: Multnomah, 2001), 17.

CHAPTER 10: WAKE UP
1. "Shock Poll: Startling Numbers of Americans Believe World Now in the 'End Times,'" Religion News Service, September 11, 2013, http:// religionnews.com/2013/09/11/shock-poll-startling-numbers-of-americans -believe-world-now-in-the-end-times/.

2. Jeff Brumley, "Global Events, Prophecy Stir Talk of 'End Times' Beliefs," *Florida Times-Union*, July 16, 2010, http://www.jacksonville.com/article /20100716/NEWS/801248442.

3. Walter Einenkel, "New Survey Shows That about 80% of Evangelicals Believe the 'End Times' Are Near," *Daily Kos*, December 8, 2015, http:// www.dailykos.com/story/2015/12/7/1457887/-New-survey-shows-that -about-80-of-Evangelicals-believe-the-end-times-are-near.

4. "The Certainty of the Second Coming," Grace to You, November 24, 1991, https://www.gty.org/library/sermons-library/66-3/the-certainty-of -the-second-coming.

5. I believe Jesus' Olivet Discourse concerns his Second Advent, not the Rapture. I believe the Rapture and the return are two phases of Christ's future coming. The Olivet Discourse addresses the signs of the Second Coming that the final generation living on earth will witness, but we can apply the same principles of alertness to our lives as we await the Rapture. For a more detailed discussion of the Rapture, see my book *The End: A Complete Overview of Bible Prophecy and the End of Days* (Carol Stream, IL: Tyndale, 2012), 121–76.

6. Grant R. Osborne, *Revelation*, Baker Exegetical Commentary on the New Testament (Grand Rapids, MI: Baker Academic, 2002), 594.

7. "Illustration: Staying Alert," *Preaching.com*, https://www.preaching.com /sermon-illustrations/illustration-staying-alert/.

8. John MacArthur, "Ready or Not—Here I Come!, Part 2," Grace to You, July 22, 1984, https://www.gty.org/library/sermons-library/2374/ready -or-nothere-i-come-part-2.

9. Ray C. Stedman, *The Ruler Who Serves: Mark 8–16* (Waco, TX: Word Books, 1976), 145–46.

10. Charles R. Swindoll, *Mark*, Swindoll's Living Insights (Carol Stream, IL: Tyndale House, 2016), 334.

11. Abraham Kuruvilla, *Mark: A Theological Commentary for Preachers* (Eugene, OR: Cascade Books, 2012), 284.

12. Ibid., 298.

13. Steven J. Cole, "Lesson 15: Are You Ready for That Day? (1 Thessalonians 5:1-8)," Bible.org, November 6, 2016, https://bible.org/seriespage /lesson-15-are-you-ready-day-1-thessalonians-51-8.

14. "Wiersbe—Story of Young Man Preaching on Last Days," Family Times, http://www.family-times.net/illustration/Last-Days/201555/.

15. Warren W. Wiersbe, *Wiersbe Bible Study Series: 2 Peter, 2 & 3 John, Jude* (Colorado Springs: David C. Cook, 2013), 69.

16. Randall Price, *Jerusalem in Prophecy* (Eugene, OR: Harvest House, 1998), 50.

17. R. A. Torrey, "Why God Used D. L. Moody," first published 1923, Wholesome Words, https://www.wholesomewords.org/biography /biomoody6.html.

18. Louis Zamperini and David Rensin, *Devil at My Heels: A Heroic Olympian's Astonishing Story of Survival as a Japanese POW in World War II* (New York: HarperCollins, 2011), 243.

ABOUT THE AUTHOR

ATTORNEY **Mark Hitchcock** THOUGHT his career was set after graduating from law school. But after what Mark calls a "clear call to full-time ministry," he changed course and went to Dallas Theological Seminary, completing a master's and PhD. Since 1991, Mark has authored numerous books, serves as senior pastor of Faith Bible Church in Edmond, Oklahoma, and is associate professor of Bible exposition at Dallas Theological Seminary. Mark and his wife, Cheryl, live in Edmond with their children and grandchildren.

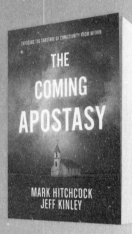

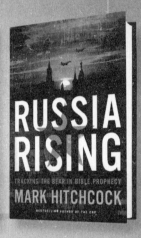
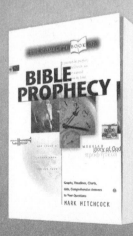